THIS IS PRO SOCCER

THIS IS PRO SOCCER

George Sullivan

Illustrated with photographs and diagrams

DODD, MEAD & COMPANY

New York

PICTURE CREDITS

Chicago Sting, Bill Smith, 80, 83; Cosmos, 2; Dallas
Tornado, 36; Ft. Lauderdale Strikers, 8, 64, Steve
Merzer, 79; German Information Center, 49, 50, 90,
104; Los Angeles Aztecs, 87, 92; Minnesota Kicks, 74;
New York Public Library, 10, 99; North American
Soccer League, 57; Portland Timbers, 78; Rochester
Lancers, C. Mason, 35 (left), 66; Royal Netherlands
Embassy, 52; Seattle Sounders, 34 (center), 94; Tampa
Bay Rowdies, Richard Steinmetz, 71, Richard Battle,
72; Washington Diplomats, 34 (right), Judy
Griesedieck, 82. All other photographs are by George
Sullivan.

**Frontispiece: Soccer calls itself "the now game." Claim
is based in part on sellout crowds like this one watching Cosmos vs. Strikers at Giants Stadium.**

1 2 3 4 5 6 7 8 9 10

Library of Congress Cataloging in Publication Data

Sullivan, George, 1927–
    This is pro soccer.

    Includes index.
        1. Soccer—United States. 2. Soccer—Canada.
3. North American Soccer League. I. Title.
GV944.U5S9   796.33′4′0973   78–10729
ISBN 0–396–07643–2

ACKNOWLEDGMENTS

The author is grateful to the many people who helped to make this book possible. Special thanks are offered Jim Trecker, Director of Public Relations, and Amy Oakley, North American Soccer League; Chuck Adams and Janie Slevens, the Cosmos; Tim Robbie, Ft. Lauderdale Strikers; Marcia Schallert, Tampa Bay Rowdies; Herb Field, Herb Field Art Studio; and Gary Wagner, Wagner-International Photos.

CONTENTS

Into the Big Time   8
Pelé—What Made Him Great?   21
A Soccer Problem   34
A Special Madness   47
How to Watch a Game   56
The Skills   75

Some of the Best   85
The Tactical Game   99
What Does a Coach Do?   108
Glossary   116
All-Time NASL Records   119
Index   123

INTO THE BIG TIME

At Lockhart Stadium one night not long ago, David Irving, a thickset forward for the Ft. Lauderdale Strikers, took a pass from a teammate, knifed his way between a pair of Cosmos defenders at midfield, then streaked for the goal. No one could stop him. From about 20 yards out, Irving fired a low shot for a score.

Then Irving, wearing a wide grin, thrust his hands over his head in a gesture of triumph.

In that moment of joy and success, Irving typified what has been happening in professional soccer in recent years. All of a sudden it is a big-time sport. Rejoicing in the manner of David Irving is very much in order.

Attendance figures for North American Soccer League games are the best evidence of what has happened. As recently as 1972, a total attendance for the year was 400,000. By 1977, the figure had jumped to more than 3.5 million, an eight-fold increase in five years. The figures included a record crowd of 77,691 who watched the Cosmos play the Strikers in a playoff game.

Other contrasts are just as startling. When the Cosmos flew back to New York after winning the Soccer Bowl, in Portland, Oregon, in 1977, having edged out the Seattle Sounders, 2-1, five thousand

David Irving gives a triumphant salute.

Yanks turn on power, but Mets still sputter
Page 67

POST SPORTS
MONDAY, AUGUST 15, 1977 25 CENTS

Jets snap slump, but Giants come up empty
Pages 62, 66

Cosmos thrill 77,691 fans

Record crowds were a leading feature of pro soccer during late 1970s.

fans mobbed the players at J. F. Kennedy Airport. It was judged to be the most excited crowd of greeters since the Beatles came to New York for the first time in 1964.

Five years before, when the Cosmos had won the NASL title for the first time, defeating the St. Louis Stars at Hofstra University, only six thousand people showed up *for the game.*

Or consider this: the Rochester Lancers paid absolutely nothing to join the NASL in 1970. Today, the Rochester franchise is said to be worth something more than $3 million.

The Lancers trained in style in San Diego in preparing for the 1978 season. Always before, training sessions had been held in Rochester, with players enduring the snow and freezing cold. And the team ate at McDonald's. "Plain hamburgers," one player recalls. "Cheese was extra."

One additional piece of evidence that soccer has

arrived came in 1978 when the Topps Chewing Gum Company announced that it was going to begin issuing soccer cards to go along with its bubble gum picture cards that feature baseball, football, basketball, and hockey players. Pictures of the soccer stars had been taken, and the statistical information to go on the back of each card had been compiled. Now there could be no doubt—soccer was "in."

"I say that in ten years soccer will be the No. 1 sport in the country and the best in the world," Phil Woosnam told *The New York Times* in 1978. Woosnam, who happened to be the commissioner of the NASL, is less than an objective source. But if soccer's future growth is at all comparable to its recent growth, then Woosnam's forecast could be right on target.

Soccer, like billiards, wrestling, and track, is one of the oldest sports in the world. About every

A soccer game in England in the early 1900s

civilization has known a ball game played with the feet.

The Greeks had a game, called *episkiros*, that was played within an area marked by boundary lines and involved both kicking and throwing a ball. The Romans are believed to have borrowed the game from the Greeks, renaming it *harpastum*. It came to be popular among Roman legionnaires and is said to have been introduced into England by them.

According to one source, the residents of the town of Derby defeated the legionnaires in a game of *harpastum* in the year A.D. 276.

Through the centuries, the sport grew by leaps and bounds. Games lasted for many hours. The goals were often located at the opposite ends of hamlets or towns. A player was permitted to kick an opponent on the shins or trip him, do anything, in fact, to keep him from getting the ball.

Rules similar to those in use today were set down in 1863 by one J. C. Thring. One of Mr. Thring's rules specified that, "Kicks must be aimed only at the ball." Another declared, "Hands may be only used to stop a ball and place it on the ground before the feet."

English settlers introduced soccer to what is now the United States during the seventeenth century, but the game's development was slow and sporadic in this country. It did find its way into schools and colleges, however, and by the 1800s was being played at Harvard, Yale, and Princeton.

Through most of Europe and in South America, it was a different story, the game showing rapid growth. An organization to govern the sport on a worldwide basis was founded in 1904. It was called FIFA, the initials standing for the French title for the organization: Federation Internationale de Football Association. By 1914, twenty-two countries belonged to the organization. Today, FIFA has approximately 140 members.

During the latter part of the nineteenth century and the early part of the twentieth century, waves of immigrants brought soccer to America. Once they arrived here, the newcomers frequently clung to the sport as they did other customs of their homelands. Soccer was a way of retaining old memories and keeping old friendships. Soccer leagues and teams were formed in immigrant neighborhoods. They carried such names as the Brooklyn German-

Empty seats were usual when New York Generals played at Yankee Stadium. Team folded in 1968.

Americans, New York Ukranians, Hartford Italians, Chicago Slovaks, and Cleveland Shamrocks.

Native-born Americans scarcely noted this activity. They were concerned with baseball, football, basketball, and, in the Northeast and upper Midwest, ice hockey.

11

During this early period, the sport of soccer was usually called football in every other English-speaking nation of the world, and *futbol* in Spanish-speaking countries. Thus, in 1913, when an organization to serve as the governing body of the sport was formed, it was named the United States Football Association. In 1945, the organization, recognizing the slow but steady Americanization of the sport, changed its name to the U.S. Soccer Football Association. Today, it is known as the U.S. Soccer Federation, a name that was adopted in 1974.

When the first attempts were made to establish professional soccer leagues in the United States, they relied on ethnic teams. The German-American League (now called the Cosmopolitan League), which is still active today, represented one such attempt, as did the American Soccer League, which was founded in 1933. Still in operation, the ASL claims to be the oldest professional soccer league in the United States.

The one-time ethnic character of the league is obvious from the names of some of the early championship teams: the Kearny (New Jersey) Irish (champions in 1934), Philadelphia Germans (1935), and the Brooklyn Hispanos (1943). As recently as 1970, the league championship was won by a team named the Philadelphia Ukranians, and in 1971 by the New York Greeks.

As these names may also suggest, the American Soccer League was for years primarily an eastern seaboard league with some teams spotted in cities of less than major league status. That's true even today. The New Jersey Americans, for example, play their home games in Wall, New Jersey. The New York franchise, with club headquarters in Manhasset, New York, uses Long Island's Hofstra University stadium as its home base.

While the league's importance has been questioned, its heritage cannot be, and league officials are proud of its "firsts." The ASL introduced indoor soccer in the United States at New York's Madison Square Garden in 1937. It became the first league in the United States to offer televised soccer when, in October, 1952, Station WPIX in New York carried an ASL game from Yankee Stadium.

It wasn't, however, until the founding of the North American Soccer League that professional soccer can be said to have moved into the mainstream of American sports. During the 1960s, the business of sports began to explode. Existing pro-

NASL commissioner Phil Woosnam

fessional leagues expanded, and new football, basketball, and hockey leagues were started. Golf and tennis were booming. Several men who were involved in other professional sports began to focus their attention on soccer. It didn't seem to bother them that native-born Americans had never cared very much about the sport.

Not one professional league, but two of them were formed in 1967, the United States Soccer Association and the National Professional Soccer League. The teams were made up of players from Europe and South America. In spite of the fact that the league received a good deal of publicity and many games were televised on the CBS network, fans stayed home. At some games, it seemed that the players on the field outnumbered the people in the stands. Millions of dollars went down the drain.

The owners merged the two leagues in 1968 to form the North American Soccer League. But even that one league proved to be one league too many. Again, the fans failed to respond. Twelve of the league's seventeen teams folded after the 1968 season, leaving only five teams, a ridiculous number for a league claiming to be of "major" status.

Phil Woosnam, a professional player from Wales who had come to the United States in 1967 to be a coach, general manager, and a player for the NASL team in Atlanta, became the league's commissioner in 1969. He was convinced that professional soccer could become successful in the United

THE DEPARTED

In the North American Soccer League's first decade of operation, teams suffered a very high casualty rate. Here are the names of those that failed during those ten years and are no longer active:

Atlanta Apollos	Detroit Cougars	Philadelphia Spartans
Baltimore Bays	Houston Stars	Pittsburgh Phantoms
Baltimore Comets	Kansas City Spurs	San Diego Toros
Boston Beacons	Las Vegas Quicksilvers	St. Louis Stars
California Clippers	Los Angeles Toros	Team Hawaii
Chicago Mustangs	Los Angeles Wolves	Toronto Falcons
Chicago Spurs	Miami Gatos	Vancouver Royals
Cleveland Stokers	New York Generals	Washington Darts
Connecticut Bicentennials	Oakland Clippers	Washington Whips
Denver Dynamos	Olympique de Montreal	

States. He had seen crowds of 20,000 attending games in Atlanta, a city with no soccer background at all.

Under Woosnam's direction, the NASL began to grow. In 1971, the league expanded to eight teams. The following year, for the first time, no franchises fell by the wayside.

Television never helped very much in selling the game of soccer to Americans. Telecasting the sport has presented problems. Because there are no time-outs as there are in basketball and football, and because there are no natural breaks in the action as there is in baseball at the end of every half inning, there are no gaps in which sponsors can insert commercials.

When CBS-TV sought to televise NASL contests in 1968, game officials were instructed to call time-outs at various periods during the game so that commercials could be run. This is standard procedure in pro football. But the interruptions destroyed the players' ability to concentrate and plan. The game that resulted scarcely resembled soccer.

Television has to adapt to soccer, not vice versa.

One agreeable solution might be for the television network to run the commercials as the game is played, interrupting the viewer but not the action on the field. As the commercial is being played, the game would be taped, then replayed for the television audience from the point where the action was interrupted. The home viewer would then be able to see the entire game, even though play would be a few minutes behind live action.

During the 1970s, soccer began to change on an amateur basis, as schools across the country began discovering the game. Young boys—and girls, too —began playing soccer by the tens of thousands. Take what happened in Dallas, for example. In 1967, there were only eleven soccer teams there. By 1973, the number had increased to 1,170 school and independent teams.

In that same period, from 1967 to 1973, the number of high school teams increased from 800 to 3,000; the number of colleges with teams, from 200 to 600.

In addition, YMCAs and CYOs, summer camps and grade schools, and park and recreation departments started offering leagues for young players. By the end of the decade, an estimated two million boys and girls were playing soccer.

All of this activity worked to the advantage of the NASL and its worried franchise holders. Young people who were playing the game wanted to watch

Soccer fans are young fans. One of every three persons attending a NASL game is a boy or girl age fourteen or younger.

good players, and so began attending NASL games, frequently bringing their parents along. Statistics show that one out of every three persons attending an NASL game is a boy or girl age fourteen or younger.

The NASL penetrated to the West Coast in 1974 and the next year expanded to 20 teams. Indoor soccer (described in the chapter titled "How to Watch a Game") was introduced that year. The NASL's championship game—between the Tampa Bay Rowdies and the San Jose Earthquakes—drew a sellout crowd, even though only 17,000 tickets were sold.

But 1975 was more important for another reason. It was the year that the Cosmos signed Pelé.

As early as 1969, when the NASL was struggling for its life, league officials pondered the idea of signing a player of international renown, someone who could make the attendance turnstiles whirl. Pro football of the day had Joe Namath, who had just led the New York Jets to a stunning Super Bowl win. In baseball, there was Tom Seaver and his teammates on the New York Mets, who had miraculously captured the World Series that year. But American soccer had no superstar and no super team.

Pelé was the only player whom NASL officials seriously considered pursuing. He was hailed as the best soccer player of his generation, perhaps the best of all time. He was believed to be the highest-

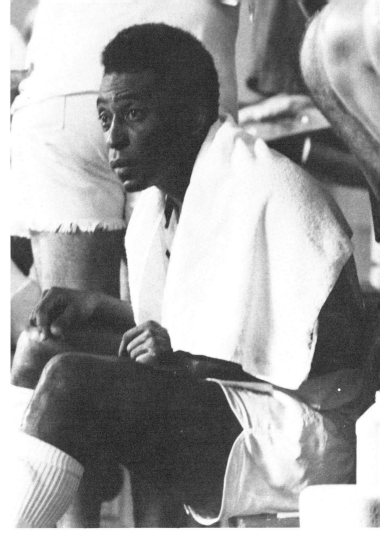

When Pelé signed with the Cosmos, it triggered period of soccer growth.

paid athlete in the world, which helped to make him a glamorous figure. His drawing power had already been established. Whenever Pelé's Santos team had toured the United States, good-sized crowds never failed to turn out to watch the Brazilian star.

During the early 1970s, representatives of the Cosmos first contacted Pelé, and asked him to begin thinking about joining the team after he retired from Brazilian soccer. Pelé's only response was a grin. Did it mean he would consider an offer from the Cosmos? Nobody knew for sure.

By mid-1974, the conversations had grown more serious. Pelé was offered $4.5 million to sign a three-year contract with the Cosmos. In October of that year, he played his final game for Santos of Brazil. Eight months later he joined the Cosmos.

Critics felt that Warner Communications, who operated the Cosmos, might have done just as well by taking the money they were to pay Pelé and flinging it down from the top of their midtown New York skyscraper into Rockefeller Plaza. But the critics were quickly silenced. Almost immediately, Pelé began to look like a bargain, even at $4.5 million.

His first game with the Cosmos was nationally televised on CBS. In Boston, Washington, Los Angeles, Seattle, and Vancouver, the Cosmos broke attendance records. The crowd of 35,620 that paid to see Pelé's first appearance in Washington established an all-time NASL attendance record (which,

of course, has been broken several times since). Everywhere the fans were affectionate and enthusiastic. Sometimes too affectionate and enthusiastic. In Boston, fans mobbed Pelé after he scored a goal, slightly injuring his ankle in seeking to make off with his shoe.

What was happening on the field was only part of the picture. Pelé went to the White House and posed for pictures with President Gerald Ford while showing him how to head the ball. Pelé appeared on the Johnny Carson show. National magazines that had never noticed soccer before featured articles on Pelé.

To put it simply, Pelé helped make soccer important in America. As Dave Anderson wrote in *The New York Times*, Pelé did for soccer what Babe Ruth did for baseball, Bobby Jones for golf, Jack Dempsey for boxing, and Bill Tilden for tennis.

Because of Pelé, other internationally known players signed up with American teams. "Pelé had to be the first," said Clive Toye, who, as president of the Cosmos, had persuaded Pelé to join the team. "The other great players around the world have to say to themselves 'If he trusts them, I have to trust them.' " So it was that England's George Best signed with Los Angeles, Italy's Giorgio Chinaglia and West Germany's Franz Beckenbauer signed with the Cosmos.

The presence of Pelé was the principal reason

that Beckenbauer joined the Cosmos in midseason 1977 instead of waiting until 1978. He felt that playing with Pelé would be an "honor," as he put it. He knew that he could not wait another year because Pelé would then be in retirement.

Soccer was growing before Pelé donned his green and white Cosmos jersey with the No. 10 on the back. But the growth the sport enjoyed during the two-and-one-half seasons that he played for them was beyond the hopes of even the most optimistic observers.

Before the 1978 season began, the NASL added six more teams, bringing the total to 24. These were divided into two conferences, and each conference was split into three divisions. This is how the teams lined up:

Each team plays a 30-game schedule. Eighteen of those games are against teams within its own conference, and 12 are against teams in the other conference.

In English soccer, not losing a game is so important as far as the league standings are concerned that teams often go for a tie and play so defensively that fans doze in the stands. The NASL has sought to avoid this by basing league standings on a point system which encourages scoring, even when a team is losing.

Each victory in league play earns a team 6 points. No points are given for a loss.

Both the winning and losing teams also receive

Presence of Pelé led to signing of Franz Beckenbauer (left), Carlos Alberto, and other international stars.

1 point in the standings for each goal scored in a game, with a maximum of 3 points to any one team. Thus, a winning team can earn as many as 9 points, but not any more than 9 points. A losing team can earn as many as 3 points.

Sixteen of the 24 teams qualify for the playoffs.

NORTH AMERICAN SOCCER LEAGUE

AMERICAN CONFERENCE

Eastern Division	Central Division	Western Division
New England Tea Men	Detroit Express	Oakland Stompers
Philadelphia Fury	Chicago Sting	San Jose Earthquakes
Tampa Bay Rowdies	Memphis Rogues	California Surf
Ft. Lauderdale Strikers	Houston Hurricane	San Diego Sockers

NATIONAL CONFERENCE

Eastern Division	Central Division	Western Division
Toronto Metros	Minnesota Kicks	Vancouver Whitecaps
Rochester Lancers	Colorado Caribous	Seattle Sounders
Cosmos	Tulsa Roughnecks	Portland Timbers
Washington Diplomats	Dallas Tornado	Los Angeles Aztecs
	Atlanta Chiefs	

The two top teams in each division—a total of 12 teams—are automatic qualifiers.

Two wild-card teams from each conference also qualify. These are simply the two teams in each conference that have the highest point total in the standings among the teams that have not automatically qualified.

The regular season and the playoffs lead to the Soccer Bowl, the face-to-face meeting of the two conference champions.

As the opening games of the 1978 season were being played, many observers speculated as to how the absence of Pelé might affect attendance figures and the success the league had been enjoying. Commissioner Woosnam had the answer. "The NASL can stand on its own two feet," he said. "Thanks to the superstar of all time, the American people now have an awareness of soccer. Pelé took us over the hurdle."

In his final NASL game, Pelé helped the Cosmos defeat the Seattle Sounders, 2-1, to capture the 1977 league championship. As the game ended, Pelé pulled off his Cosmos jersey and handed it to American-born Jim McAlister of the Sounders, who had been selected as the NASL's Rookie of the Year.

"It would be hard to find a better symbol," one reporter wrote, as he watched the god of international soccer hand over his mantle, so to speak, to the young American player.

Although Pelé's No. 10 jersey has been retired by Cosmos, the number is still seen frequently.

PELÉ—WHAT MADE HIM GREAT?

One of the nicest tributes that Pelé ever received came from an opposing player following a game the Cosmos played at Robert F. Kennedy Stadium in 1976 against the Washington Diplomats. The game attracted a turnout of 35,620, the largest crowd in NASL history up to that time. Pelé was a dominant force throughout the contest. He seemed to be everywhere at once—running, shooting, passing, dribbling, and moving his Cosmos teammates around the field with hand signals. It was a rout, the Cosmos winning, 8-2. Pelé scored twice.

When the game was over, Pelé, his dark skin glistening, sat on a stool in front of his locker signing autographs for a group of young children who crowded about him. Suddenly he looked up to see one autograph seeker who towered above all the others. It was Roy Wilner, the Washington defender who had been assigned to guard Pelé that afternoon. Pelé motioned him to come forward. He signed three autographs for the Washington player, then stood up and hugged him.

It is a rare occurrence when one professional athlete asks another for his autograph. Wilner later explained his actions to the reporters. "After what he put me through I just had to get his name on a game program," he said. "Since our coach told me last week that he was putting me on Pelé, I've had a lot of suggestions on how to stop him. I got hold

An appearance by Pelé always caused a clamor.

of some game films and studied his moves, trying to find a weakness. Believe me, it's useless. There's no way to stop that guy without knocking him out, and I'm not that type of player.

"Twice I thought I had him stopped before he

was able to start downfield, and both times he made me look like a fool. Once he went right around me, and another time he feinted in one direction and went the other way, and I found myself bumping into my own teammates," said the twenty-five-year-old Wilner, a former junior college All-American.

What skills did Pelé have that enabled him to do that to an opponent?

Moreover, what qualities did he have that enabled him to become a superstar on five continents, the richest athlete in the history of sport, and, simply stated, the greatest soccer player of all time?

Pelé was not big. He stood 5-foot-9; he weighed 165 pounds. No one could have ever said that he was successful because of his size.

He had massive thighs and a strong upper body, the muscles flat and hard.

The bone in each of his heels was exceptionally big and strong. This made him lean forward as he ran and helped him to be quick. The bone formation also acted as a shock absorber after a leap or high kick.

Layers of callus covered the soles of his feet. The toes were wedged tightly against one another. The nails were thick and yellow.

When he had to run, he could run very fast. When he had to leap, he could go very high.

He had great quickness. From a standing start, he could be at full speed in two steps. He could change direction at full speed.

He had magnificent ball control skills. When the ball came toward him, he could trap it and get it to his feet with one deft movement of his leg, thigh, or chest. He could dribble through a crowd of players, magically eluding their frantic tackles.

His passes were crisp and accurate, as if they followed a path that had been laid out on a drawing board. His shots were so powerful that when Pelé crossed the midfield line, and was still 60 to 65 yards away from the opposition goal, the goalkeeper would become wary, adjusting to guard against a Pelé shot.

His teammates praised him for his tactical skill. "A good player will be thinking one or two moves ahead," Gordon Bradley, head coach of the Cosmos when Pelé arrived there, once observed. "But Pelé can think six or seven moves ahead."

But one cannot explain Pelé's enormous success merely by counting off his physical attributes or documenting his knowledge of the game's strategy. There was much more to it—his humility and simplicity, a special magic that he had.

In Italy, Pope Pius XII gave him a special audience and a personal blessing. In Sweden, the king requested the pleasure of meeting him and shaking his hand. Newspapers in France hailed him as "an incomparable genius" and "a supreme work of art."

Children and adults idolized him, thronging about

Pelé and Cosmos teammate Giorgio Chinaglia

him for his autograph or simply to touch him. For fifteen years he reigned as soccer's king, and there were no princes.

Pelé's real name is Edson Arantes do Nascimento. He was born on October 23, 1940, in a small town in the Brazilian interior named Tres Coracoes

23

(Three Hearts), the first child of Celeste and Joao Ramos do Nascimento. Pelé's father was a dedicated soccer player, but he never played for any of Brazil's better teams.

Pelé's father was known as Dondinho. Almost all Brazilian soccer players have nicknames. As for his own, Pelé has no idea how it originated. He was about eight years old when he first began to hear it. "I have no idea where the name came from," he once said, "or who started it. As far as I know, it has no meaning in Portuguese [the language of Brazil] or any other language."

When Pelé was four, Dondinho was promoted to a team in Bauru, and the family moved there. Another boy and a girl had been born by this time, and the household also included an uncle of Pelé's and his grandmother—seven people packed into a tiny, two-bedroom wooden house.

Whenever it rained, the roof leaked. And on cold nights the entire family huddled about the wood-burning stove and tried to keep warm. While poverty was a problem for his parents, it was not for Pelé himself. "I was very happy in Bauru," Pelé has said. He had many young friends, and they played from dawn to dusk. And the game they played was soccer.

Dondinho could not afford to buy his young son a soccer ball, so Pelé and his friends would take the largest men's sock they could find and stuff it with rags or crumpled-up newspapers, form it into a ball, then tie it with string.

Pelé was ten when he and some school friends formed a soccer team. They called it the September 7th club. (September 7 is Brazil's Independence day, similar to America's Fourth of July). While the players could afford shirts and shorts, they had no shoes, so they played barefoot. Other teams in Bauru, they soon found out, were just as shoeless as they were.

Aside from soccer, Pelé disliked school. He has called himself "a total failure" as a student.

He left school to take a job in a shoe factory. His life became a daily ritual of work and soccer, soccer and work.

Pelé's coach, Valdemer de Brito, spent long hours working with him, refining his skills. By the time he was fourteen, Pelé was playing for the same team in Bauru as his father. The following year de Brito arranged a tryout for his prize pupil with the famous Santos football club. Pelé's ability to beat older, bigger players, relying on his cleverness and speed, earned him a contract with the team. His starting salary was six thousand *cruzeiros* a month—$75.

Pelé played for the Santos junior team for a time, and then was promoted to the reserve team. One day Santos was scheduled to play Cubatao, a team from a nearby town. Cubatao was not as strong a team, so the Santos coach decided to give his second stringers a chance to play. Santos won, 7-1, with Pelé scoring four goals. The Pelé legend was beginning.

In 1958, not long before his eighteenth birthday, Pelé was selected to play for Brazil's World Cup team. In a quarterfinal match, he scored the only goal in Brazil's victory over Wales. It was a goal that had to be seen to be believed. With his back to the Welsh goal, Pelé, using his right foot, suddenly hooked the ball back over his own head. As the ball caromed off a surprised Welshman, Pelé spun around and with his left foot slammed the ball into the Welsh goal for the winning score—without the ball ever touching the ground!

In the semifinals, Pelé not only resumed his wizardry but he inspired his teammates. France, Brazil's opponent in the semifinals, scored in the game's opening minutes, a goal that stunned the favored Brazilians. Pelé, the youngest of them all, gathered his teammates around him and spoke to them as their leader, persuading them to forget the damage that had been done and restoring their pride and confidence. Then Pelé went out and scored three goals, destroying the French team.

In the finals against Sweden, Pelé continued to perform in brilliant fashion. Surrounded by opposing players, he was darting away from the Swedish goal, when a pass came toward him. He stopped the ball with his thigh, and before it touched the ground he trapped it with an instep and hooked it into the air. While it hung there, Pelé whirled and clubbed the ball past the astonished Swedish goalkeeper. The shot gave the Brazilians their first World Cup.

The goal also signaled the beginning of Brazil's dominance in international soccer. The Brazilians were to win the World Cup again in 1962, and for a third time in 1970.

When the Brazilian national team was preparing for World Cup competition in 1966, Pelé was not with the team. Instead, he was miles away, in a university laboratory where medical experts were examining his slim, supple figure. His head and chest were wired for readings. His muscles were measured. His mind was probed. The tests continued on and off for three weeks. The results were always the same. "They showed," said Dr. Herman Gosling, a noted Brazilian psychologist, "that whatever field of endeavor this man entered—physical or mental—he would be a genius."

Medical tests showed that Pelé's heart pulsed at the rate of 56 to 58 beats a minute, a remarkably slow tempo. The slower one's heartbeat, the more efficiently the muscle is working. A rapid heartbeat, on the other hand, indicates that the heart is exerting itself.

The heart of the average person beats 70 to 72 times a minute. The heart rate of a person who is not in good physical condition can register 80 beats per minute or even more.

Pelé's remarkable heart and lungs enabled him to recover from an exhausting run very quickly. In the space of from 45 to 60 seconds, Pelé would be ready and able to run again while athletes who had run

Pelé demonstrates skills at Cosmos practice session.

with him would still be panting.

Pelé's field of vision was greater than the average athlete's. Most athletes are blessed with peripheral vision, which enables them to see to the side without turning the head. Otto Graham, an outstanding quarterback with the Cleveland Browns for a decade beginning in 1946, could look straight ahead and still see a pass receiver to his left or right, and throw accurately to him. Pelé had this gift, too. Tests showed that his peripheral vision was 30 percent better than that of the average athlete.

Pelé's matchless skills made him a special target during the 1966 World Cup competition. Against Hungary, he suffered a knee injury that put him out of action in a game the Brazilians lost. He returned to play against Portugal only to be brutally tackled and forced to the sidelines again. The Brazilians went down to defeat, a loss that eliminated them from Cup play. "Soccer is no longer fun," Pelé said afterward, tears filling his eyes. He told close friends that he planned to retire, but the next year he was back again.

In World Cup play in 1970, there was no stopping Pelé. He scored six times in six games to lift Brazil into the quarterfinals. His brilliant header helped the Brazilians to defeat Italy in the final, and several times he assisted his teammates on goals they scored.

The victory had more than the usual significance for the Brazilian team. The World Cup was begun in 1930, chiefly through the efforts of a Frenchman named Jules Rimet, who declared the cup which bore his name would be retired permanently by the nation that could win it three times. Brazil had won it twice and so had Italy when the two teams met in 1970.

The season of 1974 was Pelé's last with the Santos club. He retired on September 22 that year, after scoring his 1,220th goal on a penalty kick.

Years before, efforts had begun to assure that any retirement that Pelé might plan would be brief. Clive Toye, a big and burly, curly-haired gentleman, the president of the Cosmos, visited Pelé in Jamaica in 1971. Pelé was sitting near the swimming pool of the hotel where he was staying. Toye approached him. He was accompanied by Phil Woosnam, commissioner of the NASL, and Kurt Lamm, secretary of the U.S. Soccer Federation. Pelé motioned the group to sit down. Pelé's friend, Julio Mazzei, was there to serve as an interpreter.

"What we feel we need," Toye began, "is some truly big foreign soccer stars to come to the United States and popularize the game. And since the biggest man in the world of professional soccer is Pelé, we wonder if you would be interested in coming to the United States when your contract with

According to autograph dealers, Pelé's signature has more value than that of any other sports superstar.

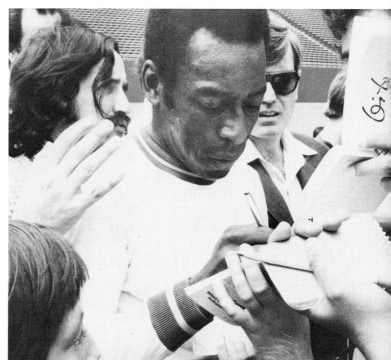

At Cosmos instruction clinics, Pelé was always a willing performer.

Santos is finished, and signing with the Cosmos."

"Tell him no," Pelé said to Mazzei.

"Maybe you'll change your mind," said Toye.

"Maybe," said Pelé, "but I doubt it."

When, in 1975, Pelé finally did change his mind, it was not merely money that made him do it. He received lucrative offers from many countries. It was something else. This is the way Pelé himself explained it: "If the offer to play had come from a team in England or West Germany or Spain, or any other country besides the United States, I would have refused. But here I might help to improve the level of soccer."

Coming from another figure, these remarks might have been taken with a shrug. But not when Pelé said them. He was sincere in the sense of mission he had about making soccer popular in the United States. He intended to work toward that goal.

Pelé's first game as a Cosmos was an exhibition on June 15 against the Dallas Tornado. The site was dilapidated Downing Stadium on an island in New York's East River. The crowd of 21,278 was perhaps one of the smallest that Pelé had seen in years, but they made up for their lack of numbers by their exuberance. Millions watched on television.

No one who saw the game could have been disappointed. Pelé assisted in the first Cosmos goal with a splendid pass right in front of the goal mouth, and later he executed a perfect header into the upper left-hand corner of the net that enabled the Cosmos to salvage a tie. Throughout the evening, he dazzled the crowd with his masterful control and precision passing. "American soccer has arrived," one television newscaster observed.

It was not merely what he could do with a soccer ball that impressed American observers about Pelé. His grace, charm, and patience were qualities that set him apart from the usual American superstar.

Although the Cosmos home games were played in a rundown stadium, Pelé did not complain. Although more than a handful of teammates lacked in skill and experience, Pelé did not sulk. "I've always been a team man, and I still am," he told the Cosmos. "Please don't expect me to win games. We must work together."

At clinics the Cosmos scheduled, Pelé was diligent and enthusiastic in instructing young players in the basics of passing and heading. No baseball or foot-ball superstar would ever be expected to do the same for his sport. "It is an exciting experience for me to see boys and even grown men—many of them discovering the sport for the first time—responding to the beauties of soccer," Pelé told sportswriter Paul Gardner.

Every time he went out onto the field it was an adventure for him. Every goal was a thrill, an

Pelé drills young player on art of pass receiving at Cosmos clinic session.

occasion to be marked by leaping high and thrusting a fist into the air.

Playing with a team such as the Cosmos in 1975 presented some problems, however. They were a thoroughly English team, as English as Yorkshire pudding. Clive Toye, the team's president was English. Gordon Bradley, the coach, was English, and so were a majority of the players.

English soccer is very different from Brazilian soccer. The English emphasize hard work and aggressiveness. With Brazilians, it's more skill and imagination. The English are more likely to follow a pattern, while the Brazilians create.

On the Cosmos, the two styles would sometimes clash. The South American players preferred to let a scoring opportunity develop slowly, nurture it, then strike. The English pressed ahead, simply, directly, with all the subtlety of a call for help. Sometimes the English players thought that the Brazilians weren't trying, weren't hustling.

There were language difficulties, too. At one time, the Cosmos players represented ten different nationalities. There were at least five different languages in use. But English was used the most. Some South Americans who didn't know English felt out of place, like they didn't belong.

The next year, 1976, it was different. Pelé and his teammates began practicing together weeks before the season opened. They played with precision and finesse from the opening day, with Pelé usually the hub of the attack. He climaxed the season with a sensational "scissors-kick" goal against Miami, somersaulting to smash a ball which was above his head into the Miami goal.

The Seattle Sounders were the Soccer Bowl champions in 1976, but the Cosmos were in the thick of playoff competition until they were eliminated by Tampa Bay in a matchup for the division title.

The next year the Cosmos could not be denied. When Eddie Firmani took over as coach in mid-season, he brought stability to the team. After finishing second in the league standings, the Cosmos swept through the playoffs and on to the Soccer Bowl to face the Seattle Sounders.

The thirty-seven-year-old Pelé played every minute of the game at top speed and when it was over and the Cosmos had won, the crowd surged out of the stands to surround him and carry him off the field. "He's going to get hurt out there," said a sportswriter.

"Are you kidding?" another replied. "Those fans would rather hurt themselves. They love him."

The love was mutual. Pelé, sitting atop the shoulders of strangers, was completely at ease, laughing and throwing kisses.

That was Pelé's last game in NASL competition. His official farewell was staged on October 1, 1977, by means of an exhibition game between the Cosmos and Santos of Brazil, the only other team that Pelé

Pelé gets treated rudely by Portland's Paul Hendrie in game at Giants Stadium.

Leaving field at game's end, Pelé grasps hands of admirers.

had ever played for. It was arranged that Pelé would play for the Cosmos in the first half and for Santos in the second half.

The day was gray and somber. It began raining early in the afternoon, but 75,646 people came, braving the downpour. Minutes before the game began, several red and white helicopters landed on an open field next to the stadium. Each brought a group of celebrities. Henry Kissinger, Muhammad Ali, Robert Redford, Barbra Streisand, and Mick Jagger were among them.

A band blared. Vendors hawked Pelé T-shirts and posters in the stands. Bedsheet banners saluting Pelé flapped in the wind.

When Pelé came out onto the field for the first time, the huge crowd stood and cheered, and thousands of fans threw confetti. Soccer teams of boys and girls presented Pelé with flowers.

Then Pelé took the microphone, and in halting English said, "I want to thank you all, every single one of you. I want to take this opportunity to ask you, in this moment when the world looks to me, to pay attention to the young of the world, the children, the kids. We need them too much. And because I think that, I believe that love is the, the, the . . ." Then his voice broke and tears ran down his face.

When he continued, the words trembled and his voice cracked: "I want to ask you—because I believe that love is the most important thing we can take from life, because everything else passes—to say with me three times, Love! Love! Love!"

Then he shouted the word three times and each time the crowd shouted it back to him. Pelé was overcome by emotion, but he managed to say, "Thank you very much." Then he put his face in his hands and wept. His friend, Carlos Alberto, once a teammate of Pelé's in Brazil, rushed over and hugged him. Then his wife and father came forward. Pelé embraced them and they held him close and cried with him. The crowd was still.

Once the game got underway, Pelé provided one last memorable moment. The Cosmos were trailing, 1-0, when, late in the first half, Pelé was assigned to take a free kick from 35 yards out. He charged the ball and sent it screaming toward the right post. It hooked inside the post by about two feet and just beyond the fingers of the Santos goalie.

The crowd came to its feet screaming. More confetti poured from the stands. It was Pelé's last goal for the Cosmos. The goal tied the score, 1-1, and the Cosmos eventually won, 2-1.

Pelé called his retirement the "most important and most saddest day of his life." The Cosmos put pressure on him to turn his back on retirement once again, offering him millions of dollars. His teammates tried to convince him to play again.

Shep Messing, the Cosmos goalie in Pelé's last year with the team, admitted that he was deeply saddened because Pelé was leaving. "I feel like quitting myself," he said.

33

Such was the effect of Pelé that not only fans but other soccer players could be saddened by his leaving. There was but one Pelé.

"We do not come for the player," a fan of Pelé's once said. "It is the man we love. He is a simple man, a nice man. He walks the streets; he picks up babies. American athletes do not do that. He, Pelé, has never lost the child in him. We love that child."

Pelé frequently plays spectator's role now. Here he watches Cosmos teammates during preseason game in 1978. Son Edson is seated in front of him.

A SOCCER PROBLEM

When the North American Soccer League announced its All-Star team in 1977, there was only one North American on it. Three Englishmen held down positions, two West Germans, an Irishman, a Welshman, a South African, and a Trinidadian. The North American player was a Canadian. There was not a single American player on the team.

But this came as no surprise to anyone the least bit knowledgeable about American professional soccer. The truth is that it is not very American.

American colleges serve as the training ground for professional football players. The same is true in basketball. Virtually every player in the National Basketball Association is a graduate of a four-year college. That's where he learns his trade.

But in professional soccer it's different. The play-

International character of American soccer is obvious from this roster of NASL stars: (left to right) Cosmos' Erol Yasin is from Turkey; Seattle's Adrian Webster, England; Tampa Bay's Derek Smethurst, South Africa, and

ers on NASL teams are predominantly citizens of foreign countries. They've been borrowed for a period of four or five months from professional teams in such countries as England, Scotland, Germany, Portugal, and Brazil. When the American soccer season is over, they return to their native countries.

Some observers criticize this policy. They say that soccer can never truly compete with American foot-ball, baseball, or basketball until the sport becomes more Americanized.

As early as 1973, many fans were led to believe that professional soccer was well on its way toward achieving Americanization. That was the year that twenty-three-year-old Kyle Rote, Jr., the handsome blond son of a former college and professional foot-ball star, soared to prominence as a member of the Dallas Tornado.

Washington's Gary Darrell, Bermuda; Rochester's John Pedro, Portugal; Detroit's Steve David, Trinidad; and Tulsa's Ninoslav Zec, Yugoslavia.

Kyle Rote, soccer's first Amercian-born superstar—almost

Kyle didn't get acquainted with soccer until he was seventeen, when he took up the sport as a conditioner for football. Dallas drafted Kyle out of the University of the South in Sewanee, Tennessee, where he had starred in soccer. But no one was prepared for the overnight success he enjoyed as a professional. He captured Rookie of the Year honors and, with 10 goals and 10 assists, also won the NASL's scoring championship, something no American had ever done (or has done since).

Rote reigned as one of the best-known figures in American sports in 1973, hailed everywhere as soccer's Great American Hope.

Then came the awakening. As NASL owners continued importing foreign talent by the planeload and the quality of play improved, Rote tumbled from his pedestal, finding it increasingly difficult to equal his performance level as a rookie. Al Miller, who became the Dallas coach in 1976, benched Rote, saying that his abilities had been "exaggerated by the media," and that "as a soccer player, Kyle Rote, Jr., is average." Thus, the designation of soccer's first American superstar was postponed.

In an effort to hasten Americanization of the sport, the NASL mandated that, as of 1978, each club must have at least six American players on its 17-man roster, and that at least two Americans must be in the game at all times. (Canadian franchises are required to sign and use Canadian citizens in these numbers.)

Furthermore, the league constitution declares that the number of American (or Canadian) players that teams have must increase on a season by season basis. By 1985, each club will be permitted to have only six foreign-born players on its roster.

The league has also sought to encourage Americanization by establishing a college draft, with club representatives meeting and choosing individual players from a pool of ready-to-graduate college talent. In 1972, the first year of the draft, eight teams selected a total of 35 American and Canadian players. But only 12 of those players were eventually signed to contracts, and only two of those players ever became regulars.

In succeeding years, the picture improved somewhat, as this table shows:

Year	Number of Clubs	Players Chosen	Players Signed
1972	8	35	12
1973	9	43	10
1974	15	60	19
1975	17	72	20
1976	20	76	30
1977	18	68	31
1978	24	96	74

At draft headquarters in New York, Cosmos coach Eddie Firmani checks selection list. Assistant coach Ray Klivecka is at Firmani's left.

While the number of college players being signed is increasing, it is still a small number. It is not going to get much bigger very soon. When a NASL team wants to improve, the coach's first inclination is to pluck a professional player off a foreign team. The quality of play in most American colleges is well below that of world-class soccer, so a pro team can't improve to any great degree by signing an

American college player. Not yet, anyway.

There are some exceptions, of course. The University of San Francisco, winners of the NCAA championship in 1975 and 1976, is one. Hartwick College (of Oneonta, New York), the NCAA champion in 1977, is another. Brown University and Southern Illinois (in Edwardsville, Illinois) are other soccer powerhouses among the colleges.

There are more, but the list is short. "The colleges are just not turning out the numbers of players that we need," Cosmos coach Eddie Firmani told a reporter for the *New York Post* in 1977. "They only play three months a year and the competition is mediocre by our standards.

"Developing kids need year-round training. Outside of the top fifteen schools, the boys are getting antiquated and ineffective coaching."

Other pro coaches tend to agree. "Sure, the quality of coaching is a problem," says Ron Newman, head coach of the Ft. Lauderdale Strikers, "but that wouldn't make much difference if young players had good competition, tough competition.

"Maybe there's another Pelé out there among American youngsters. But unless that player gets a chance to develop with a quality team in a quality league, no one is ever going to know about him."

What's said above applied to every NASL team except the St. Louis Stars. (The franchise was switched to Anaheim in 1978, to become the California Surf.) The city of St. Louis is a hotbed of amateur soccer. St. Louis University and Southern Illinois University are usually among the strongest college teams. Greg Makowski, the first player picked in the 1978 college draft, was a three-time All-American at Southern Illinois. Even the junior colleges in the area, Florissant Valley Community College and Meramec Community College, field standout teams.

Through the years, the Stars capitalized on this situation, signing many young St. Louisans. They signed so many, in fact, that they always ranked as the most Americanized of all pro teams.

The policy proved successful for the Stars. In 1975, with seven American starters on the team, the Stars won a division title. That same season, the Stars' coach, John Sewell, an Englishman with an extensive background in soccer, won the NASL's Coach of the Year award.

Sewell believes that other clubs could Americanize their teams, if they wanted to. "I'm sure that there are a lot of players in other cities who could play in the NASL," Sewell says. "But they're not getting the opportunities."

NASL teams were permitted to draft high school and junior college players for the first time in 1978. The draft that year consisted of four rounds, with each team having one selection per round. After

Greg Makowski, NASL's No. 1 draft pick in 1978, learned his soccer at Southern Illinois University, a perennial powerhouse among college teams.

four-year college players had been drafted in the first two rounds, high school and junior college players were drafted in the third and fourth rounds.

The Tampa Bay Rowdies was the first team to draft a high school player. The club chose Perry Van Der Beck of Aquinas High School in St. Louis. The eighteen-year-old midfielder had been the captain of the United States national youth team.

A total of sixteen high school seniors were picked in the draft that year. It was generally agreed that the better players among them could be successful in the pro ranks. They might not be regulars right away, but they could earn a place on the squad.

The NASL policy of drafting high school players has not made the colleges happy. They see their best potential players being drawn off by the professionals. In other sports, such as basketball and football, the professional leagues pretty much limit their drafting to college seniors.

The 1978 draft also became notable when the Cosmos picked Cleveland Lewis of Brandeis University in the first round. Lewis was the first American-born black player ever drafted by a NASL team.

The selection of Lewis called attention to an astonishing fact of life about American professional soccer—its utter lack of black players, that is, *American* black players. There are plenty of blacks in the NASL, players from such countries as Peru and Brazil, from Jamaica and Nigeria. But American blacks are as rare as Eskimos. In fact, in NASL's first ten years of operation, only one American black player ever made good. His name was Otey Cannon. He played briefly for the Dallas Tornado and the Seattle Sounders before he was released in 1974.

There are several reasons why the number of black players in professional soccer has yet to amount to a trickle. Most blacks live in the inner cities, not in the suburbs, and soccer is not an inner-city sport. There's not sufficient room for soccer fields.

"The inner-city youth looks to high-paying professional sports such as basketball and football for upward mobility out of the ghetto," *The New York Times* said recently.

Soccer could never be mistaken for a high-paying sport. The average salary of an NASL player was $19,000 in 1978. The average in baseball at the time was $76,000; in football, $55,000; and in basketball, $143,000. Such figures speak for themselves.

The New York Times also noted that soccer wasn't being televised nationally, and that "many inner-city residents see the world beyond their neighborhoods only through television."

Whatever the reason for the lack of American black participants, soccer is the poorer for it. Take what has happened in basketball. Blacks were not admitted to the National Basketball Association until 1950. In the years that followed, they quickly changed the sport. By the 1960s, a "black" style of basketball prevailed, a style that featured speed, quickness, and the leaping ability that made possible reverse layups and slam dunks. This was basketball as created in the schoolyard. In his book, *Foul!*, author Dave Wolf says that the schoolyard is the only place where young men in the slums "can move free of inhibitions and where they can, by being spectacular, rise for the moment against the drabness and anonymity of their lives."

It is a pity there are no soccer fields in those schoolyards. Think how baseball has benefited from such players as Reggie Jackson, Joe Morgan, and Rod Carew. Or think how many times pro football fans have been thrilled by O. J. Simpson or Chuck Foreman. Without black American stars, baseball, football, and basketball would be offering an inferior product. Can't the same be said of soccer?

In order to develop and become outstanding in soccer, an American player, no matter what the color of his skin happens to be, has several obstacles to overcome. One—the lack of topflight coaching—was mentioned earlier in this chapter.

The United States Soccer Federation, the organization that trains and sets standards for American coaches, has established three license classifications.

The "C" license is the lowest level; the "A" license is the highest. As of 1977, only 79 coaches held an "A" license, an average of less than two per state.

The scarcity of quality coaches isn't the only problem. Many of those coaches who are active in the sport have been criticized for the way they seek to thrust themselves into the foreground. They're overcoaching.

Under international rules, coaching is not permitted from the sidelines. There are no time-outs and only two substitutions a game are permitted. (The NASL permits a maximum of three substitutes.)

But in youth leagues and high schools in the United States, coaches *are* allowed to substitute and resubstitute as many players as they wish. As a result, there is an abundance of coaching from the sidelines, with fresh players speeding out onto the field, their heads full of strategy and instructional advice. This retards the development of a player. A young man or woman should be permitted to plan his or her own strategy, to make his or her own decisions.

American coaches have also been criticized for teaching boys and girls a game based on kicking and running. They are not being taught the many and varied skills that good ball control demands. Paul Gardner, writing in *The New York Times*, says that American youngsters are being taught an "ugly game" which he calls "bootball."

There are also problems with the rules. High school rules are different from those that college players use, and college rules are different from those in the pro ranks. For example, in high school, a team can be awarded a goal if an opposition player deliberately touches the ball. In professional play, the infraction is penalized by a free kick.

In other American sports, there is no such conflict. The rules of football that a youngster learns in high school are pretty much the same as those that are used in college and professional football. The same thing can be said of baseball.

Still another problem confronting anyone planning a pro soccer career has to do with playing facilities, specifically with the soccer fields themselves. In Europe and South America, a soccer field is used for soccer and no other sport. But in the United States, a field used for soccer may also be used for football, lacrosse, or field hockey. As a result, it is not always available to the soccer team for practice. What's even worse is that the field becomes bare of grass. Soccer as played on a dirt field is not "real" soccer. Passing and shooting are entirely different.

The size of fields available to Americans is another drawback. Most American soccer fields are laid out on the infield areas of quarter-mile tracks. This results in a field that is narrower than the

Soccer fields that young American players must use are often smaller than standard size. This one, laid out within the infield of a quarter-mile track, is typical.

standard field, and one that makes for variations in playing tactics and strategy.

Of course, there have been young men who are able to surmount all of these difficulties and attain stardom in the NASL. One such player is Jim McAlister, a defender for the Seattle Sounders, who, in 1977 at the age of twenty, was named NASL's Rookie of the Year.

McAlister never played college soccer. He did not, in fact, even play high school soccer. Yet Jimmy Gabriel, the Seattle coach, a veteran of twenty seasons in professional soccer, could say of McAlister, "The sky is the limit for the boy. Within the next couple of years, he could quite possibly be one of the best left fullbacks in the world."

McAlister started playing soccer at the age of six. He was attending Guadalupe, a Catholic school in Seattle, at the time. His father was the athletic director there. When the school's soccer team was short of players, Mr. McAlister told his son to join up.

Even though most of his teammates and the opposing players were older than he was, Jim enjoyed the experience. He was small for his age, and whenever he had tried other sports, he had come away disappointed. "When I played football with other kids, I'd go home all beat up," he says. "I didn't like that. But with soccer, I'd just go out with them and do as much as I could."

Jim developed a passion for the game, playing in

Jim McAlister, NASL's Rookie of the Year in 1977

43

open lots and city streets near his home, with players dribbling around fire plugs and parked cars. Discarded jackets and shirts marked the goals. He made rapid improvement. By the time he was thirteen, he was playing in a men's amateur league. One change was necessary. "I started out playing winger," he says. "But against the men I was too small. I was just getting kicked the whole game. After two games, the coach moved me to fullback where *I* could do the kicking."

Jim's high school didn't have a soccer team, but he continued to play amateur soccer with boys' and mens' teams. One year he played for the high school football team. He was, naturally, the team's field-goal specialist. The NASL was beginning to make itself known at this time, and Jim decided he would become a professional soccer player.

When the Sounders set up shop in Seattle in 1974, Jim, a high school junior at the time, made up his mind that he would play for the team one day. He attended every Sounder home game that season.

After he graduated from high school, Jim attended Seattle Community College. One day during his second semester there, he returned home in the evening to be told by his mother that Jimmy Johnstone, the head scout of the Sounders, had called him. "I called him back—quickly!" McAlister says. "The first thing he asked me about was my size. I was about ready to lie to him, to tell him I was 6 feet tall and weighed 250 pounds. But I told him the truth, that I was 5-foot-6 and 125 pounds."

The Sounders did not consider Jim's size—or lack of it—to be a problem. "He could really jump," Johnstone once recalled. "When heading the ball, he could beat guys who were 6 feet tall. I couldn't believe it." The Sounders offered Jim a contract in March, 1976, three weeks before his nineteenth birthday. Jim didn't hesitate. He accepted the offer and left college.

That year McAlister played for the Sounders' reserve team. Jimmy Gabriel was the reserve team coach at the time. The next year, when Gabriel moved up to take over the first team, he brought McAlister with him, and established him as the team's left halfback.

There were problems at first. Opposing wingers overpowered Jim. Gabriel wanted him to go in low for the ball, to slide if necessary, so that opponents couldn't tie him up as they had been doing. To make certain that McAlister understood, Gabriel benched him for two games.

After that, Jim played in every Sounder game, except for a two-game absence in midseason, the result of an injury he received. "We lost the two games without him," says Gabriel. "We couldn't wait to get him back."

The Sounders had a banner season, ending up in the Soccer Bowl. The Cosmos furnished the opposition. Played in Portland before a record crowd of 35,548 and another 35,000,000 watching on televi-

McAlister tunes up for game against Cosmos.

sion, the game was a thriller from the opening kickoff. But the Cosmos prevailed, 2-1. "I was sick after the game," says McAlister, "because I *knew* we were going to win. Losing was hard to take."

The game holds one happy memory for McAlister, however. Not long before it ended, McAlister spoke to Pelé, and asked him, "When the game is over, can I have your shirt?" It was Pelé's last NASL game. At the final whistle, a grinning Pelé pulled off his shirt and handed it to McAlister. "It's going into my trophy case," Jim says.

McAlister himself is quick to admit that there is no easy way to become skilled in soccer. "It's just a lot of hard work," he says. "But there's no other way. You have to go out every day on your own and work on your trapping and your heading—everything.

"But the biggest thing is to keep your pride, keep fighting no matter how much better another player may be. Don't give up. You have to *want* to play, *want* to win."

Jim McAlister's success story gives support to those professional coaches who believe that college soccer is unnecessary, that it sidetracks a young player for too long a period. A better way to learn, they say, is to sign early with a pro team.

In other countries of the world, young players are permitted to join professional teams for extended periods of schooling. In England, for instance, professional teams dip into schoolboy soccer leagues for young talent. A professional team is permitted to sign as many as forty "associated schoolboys" each year. These are young men between the ages of fourteen and sixteen who receive special coaching from the club several evenings each week while they continue their regular schoolwork.

There is no draft of college players in English soccer. There is no minor league farm system. An English pro team keeps stocking and restocking its roster from its supply of associated schoolboys.

When a boy reaches the age of sixteen and no longer has to attend public school, he is permitted to sign a professional contract. Only about one of every ten associated schoolboys is offered a contract, however.

Those who do sign with a pro team become "apprentice footballers." A young man so classified goes to live in the city where the pro team is located, the club usually placing him with a local family who can provide a home-away-from-home environment.

While the apprentice does get on-the-field experience with the professionals, he also has many training room chores to perform, such as laying out the uniforms and equipment the regular players are to wear before a game or practice session begins, and cleaning up the locker room afterward. There are several apprentices on each club and they play for the club's under-18 team. About one half of the apprentices are eventually offered contracts as professional players.

A training program of this type runs counter to what American youngsters have come to expect. After leaving high school, an American boy thinks in terms of going to college. An on-the-job training program is a concept that is foreign to most high school graduates.

Will Americans in large numbers be able to overcome this and other roadblocks that stand in their way? Are they ever going to be a major factor in pro soccer?

They can be, but there are several "ifs" involved —if playing fields and facilities are improved, if the conflicting rules and regulations that govern the sport on a high school, college, and pro level are abolished, and, most important, if more and better coaches are provided.

American youngsters have taken to soccer by the hundreds of thousands in recent years. Youth leagues are jammed in every part of the country. But whether there are large numbers of future professionals among these young players remains doubtful. Americanization is going to happen, but it is some years away.

A SPECIAL MADNESS

In English-speaking countries, it is called the World Cup of Soccer. In Spain and South America, it is El Campeonato del Mundo de Futbol. The Germans call it Die Fussball-Weltmeisterschaft. To hundreds of millions of people all over the world, it is the supreme sports event, greater even than the Olympics.

World Cup tournament competition is held every four years. The participants are the sixteen national professional All-Star teams that have survived the tournament's qualifying rounds. In 1974, Cup competition involved a total of 141 countries. That was six more countries than belonged to the United Nations at the time.

From the back streets of Marseille to the boulevards of Rio de Janiero, from Monrovia to Melbourne, the Cup matches evoke a special madness. In 1974, the final match between West Germany and Holland (won by West Germany) was played before 74,200 spectators at Olympic Stadium in Munich and relayed to 800 million television viewers around the world, the greatest number of people to watch a sporting event in history.

World Cup matches have touched off border clashes between El Salvador and Honduras. President Mobuto Sese Seko of Zaire once sent his country's team into action with the mandate to "Win or die!" (They won.) Factories have shut

This is what all the excitement is about—the World Cup.

Carlos Alberto, now a member of the Cosmos, captained Brazil's World Cup champions.

down in Brazil so that workers could watch the Brazilian team on television. In Australia, people have stayed up all night to watch telecasts featuring the Australian team when they played in Europe.

Members of teams that win the Cup are treated as national heroes, the way the first American astronauts were honored in this country. They enjoy lifelong recognition and prestige.

The idea of forming national soccer teams and conducting competition on an international basis prevailed in many parts of the world during the early 1900s. Five countries were represented by soccer teams in the 1908 Olympic Games. The number grew to 22 teams for the 1924 Games, with the United States joining in for the first time.

Even during this early period, soccer was very much a professional sport. But professional players were barred from the Olympics. Only amateurs could take part. Thus, many of the best players from such countries as England, Austria, and Hungary were unable to represent their respective nations in international play.

The Federation Internationale de Football (FIFA), in its first official meeting in 1904, had declared the right to organize an international tournament, one that would include everyone, amateurs and professionals. But efforts to launch the tournament were frustrated until 1928. That year Uruguay won the Olympic soccer title. They had also won in 1924. European soccer fans were up in arms over the success of the South Americans. The best European players, they pointed out, were professionals and thus not eligible for competition.

This dissatisfaction helped to pave the way for the first World Cup tournament, held in 1930. Several European nations—Italy, Spain, the Netherlands among them—offered to host the tournament. Uruguay wanted the tournament, too. Uruguay wanted it so desperately that the country offered to pay all the expenses of visiting teams, including travel costs, and also promised to build a new 100,000-seat stadium for the matches. FIFA officials were impressed. They chose Uruguay.

The decision offended many European nations. Only four—Romania, Yugoslavia, Belgium, and France—agreed to send teams to the tournament.

German Football Federation issued this commemorative coin in connection with 1974 World Cup finals, held in Munich. "Tip" and "Tap," mascots of the matches, were featured.

Another problem was the distance involved. This being a time before intercontinental air travel (Lindbergh had crossed the Atlantic Ocean only three years before), teams had to travel by ship. The voyage from Europe to South America took three weeks. Professional players were reluctant to fritter away so much time.

It's not surprising, then, that Europe was not represented in the Cup final match that year. Uruguay faced its neighbor to the west, Argentina. Argentina forged to a 2-1 lead during the first half, but Uruguay dominated the second half to win, 4-2. Each member of the victorious Uruguayan team was given a house by the grateful Uruguayan government.

The United States has never fared well in World Cup competition—with two exceptions. One of these exceptions occurred in the first World Cup competition.

The American team that year was made up mostly of English and Scottish professional players. Because they had become American citizens, they were eligible to represent the United States. These "Americans" were big and very strong. "We called them 'shot putters,'" Marcel Pinel, who played for the French team that year, once recalled.

The American team defeated Belgium, 3-0. They then turned back Paraguay by the same score, a victory that enabled the Americans to move into the semifinals. But that's as far as they got. A strong

Goalie Sepp Maier (left photo) and Franz Beckenbauer (far right) starred for German team, winner of 1974 World Cup.

Argentinian team dashed America's hopes with a lopsided 6-0 win.

In 1934, the World Cup finals were held in Rome, and Italy became the second host nation to win the Cup. The Italians repeated their triumph in 1938. Shortly after, World War II engulfed Europe and World Cup competition was suspended.

When the matches resumed in 1950, with the finals staged in Brazil, the United States scored one of the most astounding upsets in Cup history. The American team that year was composed of semipro players from teams in New York, Chicago, St. Louis, Pittsburgh, and Fall River, Massachusetts.

In their first game, the Americans lost to Spain,

3-1. Their next scheduled match was against England, playing in World Cup competition for the first time. The English team was led by Stanley Matthews, who, at thirty-five, was still rated as one of the most dangerous forwards in the game. England also boasted Tom Finney, described by Paul Gardner, one of the most respected soccer writers, as "perhaps the most complete all-round player ever to wear the English shirt." In their first game, the English easily downed Chile, 2-0.

So confident were the English as their match with the Americans approached, they announced they would rest Stanley Matthews, saving him for the more difficult games that were to follow. The game was played at Belo Horizonte, Brazil, on a gray day. The English players joked and laughed during the warm-ups, certain they were going to claim an easy victory.

In the minutes that followed the opening kickoff, the English forwards opened up an all-out assault on the American goal. Some shots ricocheted off the posts, others were wide by inches, while still others skimmed the top of the crossbar. The American goalie was in a frenzy, careening from one side of the goal to the other. But whatever shots didn't miss, he managed to block.

Incredibly, it was the Americans who were the first to score. Several minutes before the first half ended, Joe Gaetjens, while near to the English goal, saw a pass come toward him from a wing. He hurtled his body into the air and headed the ball into the English net.

When the teams came out onto the field to begin the second half, the English were still confident, certain that they would ultimately prevail. Though they launched one attack after another, the Ameri-

---

WORLD CUP CHAMPIONS

1930	Uruguay	1958	Brazil
1934	Italy	1962	Brazil
1938	Italy	1966	Great Britain
1942	(no competition)	1970	Brazil
1946	(no competition)	1974	West Germany
1950	Uruguay	1978	Argentina
1954	West Germany		

This powerful kick by Gerd Muller put West Germany into the lead, 2-1, just before halftime in 1974 World Cup final. The score did not change in the second half. Rund Krol is the Dutch defender.

cans somehow prevented their goal from being penetrated.

Stanley Matthews watched helplessly from the sidelines. Under the rules of soccer, substituting was not permitted. Because Matthews had not started the game, he could not play at all. As his team failed again and again, Matthews' shoulders slumped and he clenched his fists in frustration. So tightly did he clench them that he dug the fingernails into the palms without even realizing it. Only after the game was over and he looked down and saw his bloodied hands did he realize what he had done.

The single goal that the Americans scored was all that they needed. At the final whistle, spectators poured out of the stands and carried the ecstatic Americans off the field on their shoulders.

That moment has remained the high point for the United States in international soccer to this day. Not long after their miraculous victory over the English at Belo Horizonte, the Americans were eliminated by Chile, 5-2. In the years since, no United States team has been as successful as that United States squad.

In the 1954 tournament, held in Switzerland, European audiences were able to watch the matches on television for the first time. West Germany won the tournament that year.

The 1958 tournament was made notable when Brazil introduced Pelé, only seventeen at the time. The Brazilians were so masterful in attacking and controlling the ball that they made some European teams look clumsy by comparison. Brazil won the World Cup that year without losing a single match.

The Brazilians won again in 1962, and a third time in 1970. Afterward, the golden Jules Rimet Trophy was awarded the team permanently, in honor of their having captured the cup for an unprecedented third time.

During the 1970s, when soccer was mushrooming in popularity in the United States, both in terms of spectator interest and participants, Americans followed World Cup play with more interest than ever. But American teams continued to disappoint their followers.

At the ninth World Cup matches, held in Mexico in 1970, and in the tenth World Cup tournament, held in West Germany in 1974, there was no United States entry, the American team having failed to survive the qualifying rounds both times.

Nevertheless, hopes ran high as the American

Cosmos' Bobby Smith was member of U.S. squad that competed for 1978 World Cup.

53

team started out in quest of the 1978 World Cup. The final matches were held in Argentina.

The United States team was composed mostly of players from the North American Soccer League. Midfielder Al Trost, twice college Player of the Year while at St. Louis University, now a member of the California Surf, captained the team. Defender Bobby Smith, who played for the Cosmos, was the team's spark plug. Tampa Bay's Arnie Mausser was in the goal.

For the first round of competition, the United States was put into a group with Mexico and Canada. Following a round-robin series, the two teams with the best records would advance to the next round. Mexico won the series. The United States and Canada ended up with identical 1-2-1 records. To decide which team would go on to the next round, a playoff game was necessary.

The game had to be held in a neutral country. When the United States and Canada could not agree on which country, the World Cup organizers ordered them to play in Port-au-Prince, Haiti. There the two teams met three days before Christmas in 1976.

Within the game's first few opening minutes, the United States was handed two scoring opportunities. Center forward Freddy Grgurev of the German-American Soccer League got control of the ball after a frantic struggle in front of the Canadian goal. His booming shot caromed off a Canadian defender to go out of bounds over the goal line. On the

Colorful poster hailed Argentina as site of 1978 Cup finals.

corner kick that followed, forward Mike Flater of the Minnesota Kicks bounded into the air to head the ball. It went wide of the left post by inches.

Not long after, Boris Bandov, a powerfully built forward for the Seattle Sounders, got loose on a breakaway and bore down on the Canadian goalie. But he shot too soon and the goalie made a diving save.

Their two escapes encouraged the Canadians. They moved the ball with poise and assurance. The Americans seemed tense.

About midway in the first half, a crucial moment arrived. From near a touchline, Bruce Wilson, a Canadian back, hammered a 40-yard free kick toward the American goal. Mausser hurried out to make the save. But as the ball neared him, it dropped suddenly, eluding the American goalie. Brian Budd of the Canadians slammed the ball toward the empty net six yards away. Al Trost made a desperate attempt to block the shot, but the ball glanced off his thigh and into the net.

That goal set the pattern of play until the game's closing minutes. The United States team would storm down the field time after time, only to be repulsed by the waiting Canadians, who were defending with as many as eight men.

The Canadian team scored a second goal with five minutes remaining, and a third goal in the game's dying seconds. So ended America's hopes. Four more years of waiting were ahead.

Alberto Tarantini starred as defender on Argentina's 1978 World Cup winning team.

HOW TO WATCH A GAME

Try to tell someone who has no knowledge of the game how baseball is played and scored, and you'll find you've taken on a difficult task. Baseball is a complicated game and trying to explain it is like trying to explain how a fine watch works.

Soccer is different; soccer is simple. Two teams of eleven players each seek to advance an inflated ball toward the opposition goal by kicking, dribbling, and heading it. The goalkeeper is the only player permitted to use his hands.

If you only know that much about the game, you can enjoy it as a spectator. But to really appreciate what's going on, there's much more you should know. This chapter and the one that follows are meant to help you increase your understanding of the game and, thus, the amount of pleasure you get as a spectator, whether you're watching at a stadium or on television.

Many boys and girls play soccer in converted football fields, using the football sidelines and end lines as soccer boundaries. A football field is 53⅓ yards wide and 100 yards long, dimensions that make it considerably smaller than a "real" soccer field. Players are crowded together when forced to play on a field of this size, and passing and teamwork are limited as a result.

Professional soccer is played on a field that is much larger, measuring as much as 130 yards in

Official NASL ball has circumference of 27 to 28 inches, weighs 14 to 16 ounces, and features five-pointed red stars.

length and 100 yards in width. With so much territory to attack and defend, no one can kick the ball haphazardly. Instead, it must be dribbled carefully and passed from one player to another in any one of countless different patterns.

A goal, which counts one point, is the only means of scoring. For a goal to be registered, the whole ball must pass entirely over the goal line be-

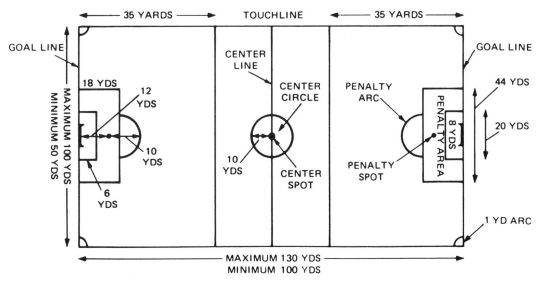

The soccer field

tween the goal posts and under the crossbar. It's different in football. In that game, when any part of the ball crosses the goal line, it's a touchdown.

Soccer games that are tied at the end of regulation play are decided on the basis of "sudden death" overtime. The game is extended by a maximum of two 7½-minute periods, a total of 15 minutes. But as soon as one team scores, that team wins immediately and no further play is necessary.

Should the game still be tied at the end of the second overtime period, the outcome is decided by means of what is known as a "shoot-out." Players on each team challenge the opposing goalkeeper in exciting one-on-one competition.

The visiting team is given the ball on the opposing team's yellow line, that is, at a point 35 yards from the goal line. Attacking players have five seconds in which to take a shot. If the shot is missed, then it becomes the other team's turn. The teams take five such shots alternately.

If the score remains tied after each team has taken five shots, the teams continue shooting alter-

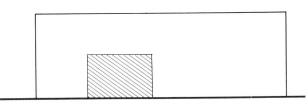

Soccer goal is eight times bigger than goal in ice hockey (shaded area).

nately until one team has scored.

The goal in soccer is very big—at least it is as compared to one in ice hockey. The two upright posts are 8 feet high and 8 yards apart. In hockey, the goal is only 4 feet by 6 feet. This means that the goalie in soccer has *eight times* as much area to defend as his counterpart in ice hockey.

Only the goalkeeper is permitted to touch the ball with his hands, and he may do so only when he is within the penalty area, a rectangular area in front of the goal that measures 18 yards by 44 yards. When the goalie is within the penalty area, he is also permitted to hold and carry the ball, providing that he bounces it every four steps.

The rules are enforced by three officials; a referee and two linesmen. The referee is in charge; his decisions are final. The linesmen—one is stationed along each of the touchlines (sidelines)—indicate where the ball goes out of bounds, watch for offside violations, and award throw-ins and corner kicks (terms that are explained below).

A game is 90 minutes long, divided into 45-minute halves. The tempo of the game is different from most American sports. In baseball, time is no factor at all. The game continues until nine innings have been completed, no matter how long it may take. Players frequently stand around doing nothing.

As for football, it's not the action-packed game

A referee (right) and two linesmen enforce the rules.

that many people claim it to be. It's been found that in the average football game, which consumes about 2¾ hours of clock time, features only about 10 minutes of actual play. The rest of the time is spent huddling, lining up, and marking the ball. Football also has countless time-outs.

But in soccer the clock runs constantly and so do

An official checks net before a game.

the players. There are no time-outs.

Players have to learn to pace themselves. A team that goes all-out during the first half may become so fatigued that it comes apart in the second half.

Other aspects of the game are as follows:

THE KICKOFF—A flip of a coin decides which team will kick off. The team losing the toss gets to choose which side of the field it will defend.

Each team lines up within its own half of the field. The referee places the ball on the center spot. One player is assigned to be the kicker. Opposing players must stay at least 10 yards from the ball as it is kicked. It's for this reason that a center circle with a diameter of 10 yards is marked on the field.

The referee's whistle blasts. The kicker boots the ball to a teammate who must be within the opposition's half of the field when he receives it. The ball doesn't have to travel far on the kickoff, only "the distance of its own circumference," says the rulebook. This is a mere 27 to 28 inches.

A kickoff also takes place after a goal has been scored. The team that has been scored upon does the kicking. And there is a kickoff at the beginning of the second half. If Team A kicked off to begin the game, Team B kicks off to start the second half.

SUBSTITUTING—If you play high school soccer, the rules undoubtedly permit free substitution, which means that a rested player can be sent into the game at almost any time. But in pro soccer, free substitution is not permitted. Teams are allowed only three

Patrolling the sideline is no easy job.

substitutions per game, the goalie and two other players. There are no exceptions, not even in the case of an injury. Should a team have used up its substitutes and then a player suffers a serious injury, breaks a leg, say, and is forced to leave the game, the team must play one player short.

Or suppose a player is ejected for what the rulebook calls "violent conduct." If his team has used up its quota of three substitutes, no replacement can be sent in. The team must play the rest of the game short-handed.

OUT-OF-BOUNDS PLAY—When the ball goes out of bounds, as it does with some frequency, it is put back in play by one of three methods: a throw-in, a corner kick, or a goal kick.

A throw-in occurs when the ball goes out of bounds over a touchline, that is, a sideline. If a player from Team A touched the ball last, a player from Team B is awarded the throw-in from the point where the ball crossed the line.

In executing a throw-in, a player must use both hands, and deliver the ball from behind and over his head. Both feet must be on the ground. If the player violates either of these two rules, the ball goes over to the other side for a throw-in.

A throw-in can lead to some exciting moments. Although a player is not permitted to throw the ball into the opposition goal, with a long throw he can sometimes put the ball into the opposition goal area (the 6-yard by 20-yard rectangle in front of each

Chicago's Alex Skotarek gets set to throw to Gene Strenicer.

Plenty of power goes into the corner kick.

goal) and that often leads to a scoring opportunity.

Of course, the defensive players are going to try to outwit any such strategy. Having a one-player advantage, they can post two men at the expected point of attack.

When the ball goes over the goal line, and is last touched by a member of the defending team, the attacking team is awarded a corner kick. It's taken from the corner area closest to where the ball crossed the goal line.

Furious action usually occurs on a corner kick, since the attacking forwards are all within scoring range. The rules permit a goal to be scored directly on a corner kick, but this seldom happens. Usually the ball goes to another player who attempts to boot it in.

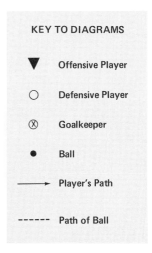

KEY TO DIAGRAMS

▼ Offensive Player

◯ Defensive Player

⊗ Goalkeeper

● Ball

——— Player's Path

------ Path of Ball

When executing a corner kick, an experienced player can make the ball swerve toward the goalkeeper or away from him. The goalkeeper can usually cope with a ball that's curving toward him, but one that swerves away can be a problem. It can tempt the goalkeeper to come out of the goal, which gives the onrushing forwards a golden scoring opportunity. And since the ball is swerving toward the shooter as he dashes in, he can drive the ball with great power.

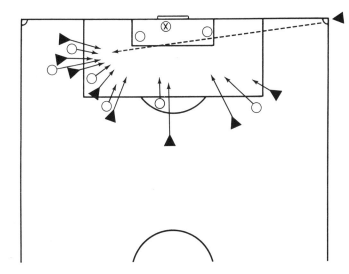

Teams have set plays to use in corner-kick situations. One such play calls for four or five attackers to await the kick just inside the penalty area at the far end of the goal. As soon as the ball is kicked, the players surge toward it, hoping by the sheer force of their numbers to get a shooting opportunity.

Another corner-kick play begins with a short kick. It is designed to force the defending players

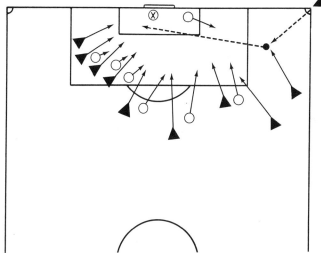

to move away from the goal. As soon as the defenders begin to move out, the player who has received the kick lofts the ball to several of his teammates clustered at the far side of the goal. They surge forward in an attempt to rap the ball in.

The goal kick is the third method of putting the ball in play after it has gone out of bounds. The goal kick is taken by a member of the defending team after the ball has gone over the goal line and was last touched by a member of the attacking team.

Charging from behind could be the ruling here. A direct free kick would be the result.

The term "goal kick" is rather misleading. The ball is not kicked toward one's goal, but away from it. It's first placed down within the goal area, then booted upfield. The team's most powerful booter does the kicking. Usually it's the goalie or a fullback.

It's always a high and lofted kick—and one that's carefully placed. An outside forward is frequently the target.

FOULS AND THEIR PUNISHMENT—Anyone who is the least bit familiar with soccer knows that you can't touch the ball with your hands. But that's only one of the game's serious crimes. Most of the others involve contact between opposing players.

When one player has the ball in his possession, the rules permit an opponent to shoulder-charge him in his effort to take over the ball. Outside of that, little else in the way of contact is permitted. Holding, pushing, striking, kicking, tripping, jumping at, or violently charging at an opponent are all serious offenses.

The penalty in each case is a direct free kick. The kick is taken from the spot where the foul took place. It's called a *direct* free kick because a goal may be scored directly from the kick.

Of course, whether it's possible for a goal to be scored depends to a great extent on where the foul occurred. It has happened that a player has charged into the opposing goalkeeper and the goalkeeper's team is then awarded a direct free kick. But aside from giving the team possession, what good is it?

The opposition goal is more than 100 yards away. There's not the slightest chance that a goal is going to result from the kick. Some observers say that the rules are flawed in this respect and should be rewritten.

When the rule infraction takes place within 25 or 30 yards of the offending team's goal, the situation is entirely different; a goal can be the direct result.

As the referee is placing the ball down, defending players, as many as four or five of them, stand side by side to set up a wall between the ball and the goal. This calls for counterstrategy by the offense. The kicking team has three choices: to try to go through the wall, go around it, or go over it.

Going through the wall means exactly that, kicking the ball so hard that it blasts through a gap between players. This is unusual in professional soccer, however. Players have no fear of the ball; they'll stand firm in the face of the hardest cannon shots. No one moves; no one tries to duck.

Going around the wall, while more difficult, is more likely to pay off. In the situation diagrammed at left below, the player taking the direct kick boots the ball to a teammate on the left side of the wall, then races to the right for a return pass, which sets up a clear shot at the goal.

Going over the wall can be effective, too, although it requires a skilled kicker. As shown below, the kicker lofts the ball over the wall toward the far goal post, beyond the reach of the goalkeeper. Either of

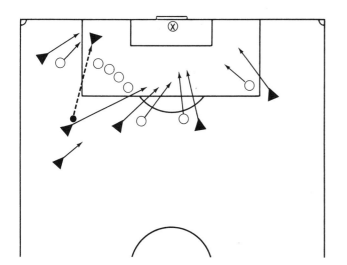

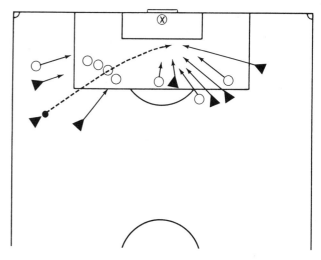

Goalkeeper Jack Brand braces for a penalty kick.

two or three attacking players then have the opportunity to dash in, outjump the players who are guarding them, and try to head the ball into the goal.

The penalty kick, one of soccer's most dramatic moments, is a special type of direct free kick. It occurs when any one of the offenses mentioned above—holding, pushing, or striking an opponent, and the others—is committed within the penalty area, that 8-yard by 20-yard rectangle in front of the goal. The penalty kick is taken from the penalty spot, a mark 12 yards away from the goal and directly in front of it.

Only the goalie may defend against the shot. All other players must leave the penalty area. In addition, the goalie is not permitted to move until after the ball has been kicked. If you think that these rules make it difficult for the goalkeeper to stop the shot, you're right. Saves seldom happen on penalty kicks. In fact, in professional soccer, a goal scored on a penalty kick is almost as certain as a point-after-touchdown conversion in professional football.

Every team has a penalty-kick specialist, a player with a booming shot and a killer instinct. He makes up his mind in advance as to the type of kick he's going to execute and decides where he's going to place it. One secret of success is not changing your mind once these decisions have been made.

Some goalies, before the kick is to be taken, move more to one side of the goal. What they're hoping to do is tempt the kicker to aim for the wider side—and then they dive for that side the instant the ball is kicked. Other goalies decide in advance as to where they think the ball is going to go, and then simply dive toward that side at the kick. This strategy can make the goalie look a bit silly—or make him a hero. Indeed, sometimes the goalie guesses right and makes a spectacular save.

When the penalty kick is about to be taken, players on opposing teams align themselves as shown here. Everyone on the field has to stay alert to play the rebound that may carom off the crossbar or one of the goal posts. Defensive players are ready to surge toward the goal after the shot, ready to aid their goalkeeper in case the ball bounces free.

Shep Messing, now goalkeeper for the Oakland Stompers, once demonstrated a unique method of dealing with penalty kicks. This was in 1972 when

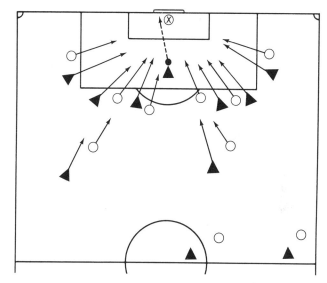

On a penalty kick, teams line up like this.

Messing was Harvard University's goalkeeper and a member of a squad of Olympic hopefuls. The elimination matches came down to a final game in Kingston, Jamaica, between the United States and a team representing El Salvador. The winning team would go to the Olympic Games in Munich. The losing team would read about the Olympics in the newspapers.

At the end of the game, the score was tied 0-0. Overtime failed to break the deadlock. Under the rules that prevailed, five penalty kicks by each team were to decide the outcome. Nine kicks were taken.

The United States made five of them, El Salvador made four. Now it was El Salvador's turn to take its fifth kick. The game rested on its success or failure.

As the El Salvador player was lining up to take the shot, Messing paced back and forth in front of the goal. Suddenly he stripped off his jersey and charged at the astonished El Salvador player. He flailed away at him with his jersey as he screamed fiercely, "Eeeeeeeee-yah! Eeeeeeeee-yah!" The El Salvador player cowered in fright.

Then, just as suddenly as he had bolted toward the player, Messing turned and walked calmly back to the goal. He took his stance, and said, "Ready."

The El Salvador player got set. He approached the ball coolly—then blasted it two feet over the crossbar.

For infractions of the rules that are less serious than those cited above, an indirect free kick is awarded. The ball is again placed down on the spot where the infraction took place. A goal cannot be scored from the kick; it must be played by another player after it is kicked.

An indirect free kick is awarded when the goalkeeper, while holding the ball, takes more than four steps without bouncing it. Offside violations or instances of what the referee judges to be "ungentlemanly conduct" also result in the awarding of an indirect free kick.

The strategy on such plays is for the player doing the kicking to deftly slip the ball to a teammate, who then fires at the goal. Of course, the strategy used depends on the field position of the attacking team. It sometimes happens that the team is so far away from the opposition goal that no real attempt toward achieving a score is possible.

In his breast pocket, the referee carries two plastic cards, each about the size of an ordinary playing card. One is yellow, the other red.

When the referee spots a foul, he blows his whistle. Play stops. If the player who has committed the foul has been persistently breaking the rules, the referee holds the yellow card commandingly in the air. This is a signal that the guilty player is being cautioned. In addition to the caution, the opposing team is awarded an indirect free kick. Protesting any decision of the referee's can also cause a player to be cautioned, as can what the rules call "ungentlemanly conduct."

If the referee flashes the red card, it's more serious.

Referee flashes red card (left) for serious infraction; yellow card is caution card.

It's a signal the player is being ejected. A player is sent off the field if he persists in misconduct after first being cautioned, or if he is guilty of "violent conduct," which includes the use of foul or abusive language.

THE OFFSIDE RULE—Unless you've played some soccer yourself, the game's offside rule may cause you some difficulty. First, understand why such a rule is necessary. It was brought into being to prevent "goal hanging," the practice of one or more players staying within the very shadow of the opposition goal, waiting for a pass and the opportunity to score. If such a situation were allowed to exist, soccer wouldn't be much of a game.

Hockey has an offside rule that is somewhat similar to soccer's, and, in basketball, there's the three-second rule, which prevents a player from standing near the basket waiting to be fed. (The rule states that a player cannot remain within the free-throw lane for more than three seconds.)

In soccer, for a player to be offside, three conditions must be fulfilled as the ball is being passed to him:

1. He must be ahead of the ball, that is, nearer to the opposition goal than he is to the ball.
2. He must be within 35 yards of the opposition goal.
3. There must be fewer than two opposing players between him and the goal line.

The second of these conditions is common only

Flag marks pro soccer's offside line.

to professional soccer. In amateur play, the rules state that an offside infraction can occur anywhere within the opposition's half of the field. The NASL introduced the 35-yard-line rule in 1973. To help officials enforce the rule, two white lines are drawn across the field, each 35 yards from a goal, and yellow flags mark the line at each end.

The 35-yard line was introduced to open up the game and make it more exciting. It *has* changed the game, but not very much.

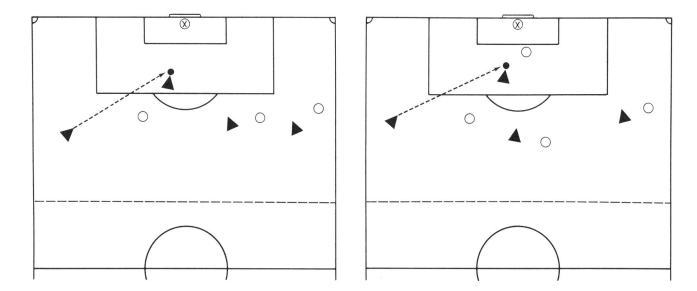

Player receiving pass is offside in diagram at left; there's only one defensive player positioned between him and the goal (the goalkeeper). Horizontal broken line represents 35-yard line, the offside line. In diagram at right, there is no offside violation, since two defensive players are between player receiving the ball and the goal.

An offside violation is often difficult for the referee to detect. He can't blow his whistle unless he's sure that the ball is ahead of the player who is to receive the pass, that is, the ball is nearer to the goal than the receiver. Nor can an offside infraction be called if the ball was last touched by an opposing player. The offside rule also does not apply if the player receives the ball directly from a throw-in, corner kick, or goal kick.

It is possible for a player to be technically offside, yet the referee doesn't call an infraction. This happens when the referee judges that the player has gained no advantage by being in what amounts to an offside position. The pass may never get to the man or the play may suddenly shift to the other side of the field.

While not every fan realizes it, American professional teams are out of step with the rest of the soccer world in that games are played in the spring and summer. American high schools and colleges play their games in the fall. And through most of Europe, soccer is a winter game. (Winters are milder in Europe than they are in the Northeast and upper Midwest sections of the United States.)

But the NASL is in the process of making professional soccer a wintertime activity through its indoor version of the game. Indoor soccer isn't something new. The NASL has been conducting indoor championships since 1972. Games are scheduled in January and February.

Indoor soccer is a much different game than the outdoor version. Indeed, it's said to resemble ice hockey more than it does the traditional brand of soccer.

Indoor soccer is played on a court the size of a hockey rink, which measures 85 feet by 200 feet. Walls surround the playing surface to keep the ball from going out of bounds.

Each team is composed of six players, including a goalkeeper.

The goals are 4 feet high and 16 feet wide.

The game is played in three 20-minute periods and fouls are penalized by suspending the guilty player for from two to five seconds. During the time he's sitting out his penalty, his team must play short-handed.

Indoor soccer is played on artificial turf. But it has a much shorter nap than the artificial turf used

Indoor soccer field resembles hockey rink. Here Tampa Bay Rowdies face Washington Diplomats.

In indoor soccer the goalie is under heavy and constant pressure.

outdoors for football or baseball. This, plus the fact that it's usually laid down over ice, hardwood, or cement, makes for an extremely fast playing surface. It's also an abrasive surface. An enthusiastic tackle can leave the tackler with a rug burn the size of a dinner plate.

The boards that surround the court can be another hazard. "The boards work for you on defense," one player points out. "When you put a man into the wood, there is no way that he can keep control of the ball."

The boards can also be used in passing, with a player caroming the ball off them to be picked up by a teammate, or he can even act as his own receiver.

Only when the ball goes into the stands, as it does occasionally, is it considered out of bounds. If the ball doesn't come back quickly, the crowd begins chanting, "Throw it back! Throw it back!"

As these paragraphs suggest, indoor soccer is much faster than the outdoor game. Since the ball is always in play, unless kicked over the wall, there is hardly a moment for a player to catch his breath. "After three or four minutes, your legs feel like Jell-O," one player recalls. "That's because there's no letting up. I'm a striker; I never thought of myself as a defensive player. But in the indoor game, I must get back as fast as I can, and at least get in someone's way. I'm running all the time."

Most players are exhausted after just a few minutes of play. For this reason, the rules of indoor soccer, like the rules of hockey, permit free substitution.

Players can't relax when the ball misses the goal and goes beyond the goal line. Instead of going past the line, the ball rebounds off the boards and can be kicked again by the shooter or one of his teammates.

"You have to have an entirely different style when you play indoors," says one goalie. "The ball comes at you from every direction, with many different people kicking it. When a shot is wide, you have to go wide with it and trap it against the boards. Otherwise, it can come back to torment you."

Being a goalie in indoor soccer can be discouraging. The number of goals per game are evidence of this. Scores of 12-9 and 14-7 are typical.

While indoor soccer had little impact upon the American sports scene during the decade of the 1970s, many people believe the game has a bright future. Goalies of the world can't be too happy about that.

Pro players can trap the ball and drop it to their feet in the blink of an eye. Trapper here is Ade Coker.

THE SKILLS

In the opening round of the World Cup finals in 1970, Brazil vs. Czechoslovakia, the great Pelé, running at full tilt, trapped a swerving 40-yard pass with his chest; and then, without breaking stride, let the ball fall to his feet and slammed it into the net. It all happened within the blink of an eye.

For sheer ball control, Pelé had no equals. That fact alone could explain his enormous success, for ball control is soccer's essential skill.

A professional player is able to make the ball do whatever he wants it to do—without using his hands, only his legs, feet, body, and head.

The first object in achieving control is to get the ball to your feet. This involves trapping it, that is, killing the ball as it comes toward you.

Professional players are able to receive and trap the ball instantly and totally. There's no jiggling or jerking when the ball arrives. Bang! It's dead!

Of course, the specific method a player uses in trapping the ball depends on how the ball comes to him. From what direction is it coming? How far off the ground is it? If the ball is a high line drive, he'll use his head or a shoulder. If the ball is descending, as when it arrives, he'll trap it with his chest. A thigh, a shin, an instep, the inside of the foot, the outside of the foot, or the sole of a shoe can be used in trapping the ball.

Trapping is not a natural skill for Americans. It is, however, for many foreign-born players. Throw an American boy a ball and he'll put out his hands to catch it. This is because of his early experience with a baseball, basketball, or football—all balls that are meant to be thrown and caught. But throw a ball to a European boy and he'll stop it with a foot or thigh or some other part of the body. Americans do become skilled in trapping the ball, but it takes determination, plus the hard work that determination implies.

Once the player has the ball at his feet, he then wants to get rid of it, that is, to pass the ball to a teammate or shoot it. The basic skill in passing and shooting is, of course, the kick.

Professional soccer players have as many as twenty different ways of kicking the ball. When a player wants to kick a short pass to his left or right, he uses the appropriate side of his foot. To get power into his kick, he'll point the foot down and swing the bony instep into the ball.

At one time or another during a game, every part of a player's foot is likely to be used in executing kicks—except the toes. When you use the toes, you can't fully control the ball. Also, toe kicks executed while wearing soft, lightweight soccer shoes can be painful.

A player controls the ball's trajectory by the way he positions his body as he kicks. He knows that if he places his nonkicking foot alongside the ball and keeps the knee of his kicking foot over the ball, the

Professional players have at least twenty different ways of kicking the ball. Here Clive Griffiths of the Chicago Sting shows a part of his repertoire.

result will be a low, line drive, a real grass cutter.

To get the ball up in the air, to loft it, the player plants his nonkicking foot to the side of and in back of the ball, and he leans back, so that the foot slips underneath the ball as he kicks. In American pro football, the place-kicker attempting a field goal approaches the ball in much the same fashion, leaning back as he boots. What he's trying to do, of course, is to get the ball up in the air and over the crossbar.

Lofted kicks in soccer are somewhat rare, it must be said. The goal's crossbar is 8 feet above the ground, so kicks directed toward the goal never have to be any higher than that. When passing, a high kick takes too long to come down, giving an opposing player the time to cover the intended receiver.

The soccer player also knows he can control the ball's flight by the way in which he makes contact with it. If he makes contact to the right of center on the ball as he swings his instep through, he knows the ball will curve to the left. If he kicks hard enough, the ball will not merely curve, it will swerve viciously.

Most amateur players have a "natural" foot when it comes to kicking the ball, a foot that they favor. This limits their effectiveness. A kicker who is naturally right-footed and inept with his left foot is going to be limited in the amount of kicking he can do anytime he has a sideline close to his left side. Professional players have no such difficulties. They are equally skilled with either foot.

There can be times during a game that professional players won't even bother trapping the ball before shooting or passing. They'll simply kick the ball on the fly; they'll volley it.

Any kind of volley is a dangerous shot. There's simply no time for the defensive player, usually the goalie, to get set to block it.

Besides its value as an offensive weapon, the volley is useful defensively. When a defensive player sees the ball coming toward him while he's near his own goal, and he is under pressure from the attacking team, he can use a volley to clear the ball.

A player can volley with the side of his foot or his instep. What's difficult about volleying is getting in position before the ball arrives. Pinpoint timing is vital, too.

The overhead volley is one of soccer's more advanced techniques. Your back is toward the ball as it comes your way at about shoulder level. You throw your legs into the air, driving the ball back over your head with an instep. You have to get your head and shoulders out of the ball's path, and the only way to do this is by falling backward. This means, since you land on your shoulders, that the overhead volley can be a painful piece of strategy.

Dribbling is a skill that allows a player to keep possession of the ball—keep control of it—as he runs. Players not only have to know how to dribble, sometimes daring an opponent to take the ball, then streaking away with it, they also have to know when to dribble. This is a common failing among beginning players. They dribble too much, which slows down their team's attack. A dribbler always runs the risk of losing the ball to an opposing player.

A skilled player will dribble only in certain situations. He knows that a pass, since it travels faster than he can ever hope to dribble, is the better weapon.

Portland's Brian Gant (16) screens the ball from Graham Oakey of the Washington Diplomats.

Of course, dribbling is what a player will do when he wants to attract a defender. When the defensive man moves to cover him, a teammate is likely to be left unguarded. Then the dribbler can send the man a pass.

When a player is on a breakaway and there's only one defender between him and the goal, a smart dribbler will keep possession of the ball, not pass it. The dribbler has the advantage in such situations. He knows what he's going to do with the ball; the defender can only guess what's going to happen. It's something like the situation in American football when a pass receiver makes a catch and then gets loose in the open field. It's very difficult for one man to bring him down.

Sometimes a player who is dribbling finds his path blocked by an opposing player. He tries to fake him out of position but he can't. To keep advancing the ball, he turns sideways and dribbles with the foot farthest from the defender. This enables him to keep his body between the opposing player and the ball. This tactic is called screening.

England's Stanley Matthews, who was dubbed a knight of the realm by Queen Elizabeth II, the only soccer player to be so honored, has been called the best dribbler in soccer history. He used his skill to force the player covering him into desperate, even foolish, moves. It wasn't until he was thirty-five, in 1950, that Matthews played on a World Cup team for England. By then, the game was changing, with more and more emphasis on team play. Yet Matthews' talent was of such proportions that he still proved to be a dominant force.

Heading, hitting the ball with one's head, is, like trapping, another skill that Americans have to work hard to develop. In football, when the ball comes toward your head, you reach up and catch it. In baseball, if you're batting, you duck. Only in soccer is the head used as a hitting instrument.

It takes a certain attitude to be successful as a header. Being tall doesn't necessarily help. Being short is no drawback. What heading requires is a

To be successful when heading, you must attack the ball. Ft. Lauderdale's Ray Hudson demonstrates.

sense of timing and an aggressive manner. You have to want to go and get the ball, want to attack it. What you must never do is let the ball attack you.

The ball is headed from the center of the forehead. But it's not just the forehead that does the work. As the ball approaches, the player crouches, then springs forward to meet the ball, snapping the head forward so that the powerful muscles of the neck and shoulders are brought into play. It's like delivering a punch with the head.

It's usual for one to head the ball from amidst a crowd. Thus, body contact is frequent when you're a header.

Players head the ball for the same reasons they kick it—to deliver a pass, to attempt to score, or to clear the ball. Not only do they jump to head the ball, but they head on the run and then there is the spectacular diving header. In this, the player travels through the air like a dart to nail the ball with his forehead. It's not a skill the beginner has to be concerned about.

"Don't close your eyes when you head the ball," say the instruction books. But top players readily admit that at the moment of impact their eyes do blink shut. There's nothing that you can do to prevent it.

The rules of soccer do allow body contact, but there are definite limitations as to how that contact can be made. You cannot charge an opponent from behind. You cannot use your elbows or hips when

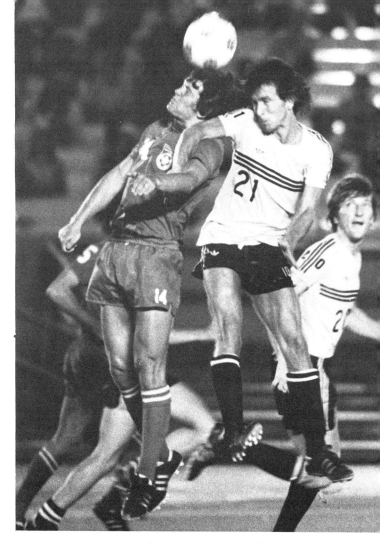

Do pro players shut their eyes when they head? Camera confirms that they do.

you charge. What you can do is charge an opponent who is in possession of the ball, your shoulder striking his. In so doing you must be attempting to gain possession of the ball. You are not permitted to deliver a shoulder charge just to shake up an opponent.

A player who charges an opponent simply for the sake of charging, or charges an opponent from behind under any circumstances, is guilty of a foul. The penalty is a direct free kick. Should the infraction take place within the penalty area, the penalty is a penalty kick. That's heavy punishment. But the harshness of the penalty does not prevent soccer from frequently being a rough-and-tumble sport. Shoulder-charging the player with the ball gives ample opportunity to deal out punishment, if that is what one is intent on doing.

The shoulder charge is one of soccer's two basic defensive tactics. The other is the tackle. In soccer, tackling means using your feet to take the ball away from an opponent.

A player can tackle from the front, first blocking the ball, then sweeping it away. There is also the sliding tackle, used by a defender who wants to stop a player who has broken into the open and perhaps is in shooting range. It's executed from the side and in much the same manner that a baseball player slides into second base, the player flinging himself feet first to the ground and reaching out with the toe of one shoe.

Victim of an enthusiastic tackle, Cosmos Franz Beckenbauer goes head over heels.

A goalie's success depends on how well he can use his hands, not his feet. This is Eric Martin of the Washington Diplomats.

One's timing has to be perfect. If the defender slides too early, the player with the ball can swerve around him, leaving the tackler sitting there. If the tackler slides too late, he runs the risk of hitting the legs of the man who has the ball. The referee's whistle sounds; a free kick is the result.

Tackling, heading, trapping, and dribbling are the skills that every player must have—except the goalkeeper. He doesn't even have to do much kicking, at least not the kind of kicking that attacking and defending players have to do. His success depends on how well he is able to use his hands, on how surely he catches the ball. And when he can't catch the ball, he has to be able to tip it or punch it away.

Being a goalie is the toughest job in soccer. After a game, his head aches from being kicked by opposing players. Welts and bruises cover his upper body. His hands, unless he wears protective gloves, are likely to be scraped raw.

Besides the physical punishment, there is the emotional strain. "It's always intense," says Shep Messing of the Oakland Stompers. "Sometimes I'm exhausted just from following the ball for 90 minutes. And even when the team scores, I can't allow myself any emotion. The only feeling I have is of relief, relief that play has paused for a moment."

The goalie has to be able to gather in ground balls, being sure to back up his hands with his feet as he does so. He has to be able to put away balls

When he can't catch the ball, the goalkeeper has to be able to tip it away. Chicago's Merv Cawston does the tipping here.

that are aimed at his chest. When the ball is driven toward the goal and is above his head, he has to be able to leap high and deflect it away. He has to be able—and willing—to make diving saves, leaping across the goal mouth.

While the goalkeeper is generally regarded as a defensive player, he has many offensive responsibilities. After he's got the ball in his hands, he has to get rid of it. If there's a teammate nearby who is open, he is likely to throw him the ball. He uses an

83

overhead motion. The rules allow him to take four steps before he fires. When a teammate is *very* close, the goalie may roll the ball to him.

If there is no one to throw to, the goalkeeper then kicks the ball, punts in the same way a football player punts a football, booming the ball down the field. The difference is that he targets on a teammate. Punts of 50 or 60 yards are frequent in professional soccer.

As these paragraphs suggest, a goalie has to be multitalented. He also has to have a good amount of courage. And it takes one other quality, a sense of where and how to position oneself in relation to the goal.

Some goalies make their job look easy. The ball always seems to come right to their hands. Other goalkeepers are forever leaping and diving to make saves. While the acrobats are likely to be talented, it can be that they're constantly getting caught out of position. The goalie who seldom has to move to get the ball has mastered his trade by virtue of his positional sense.

Most goalies take up a basic position in the center of the goal and about one yard in front of the goal

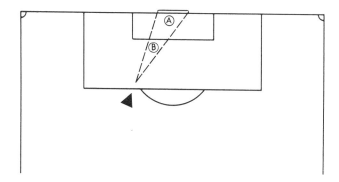

By leaving goal and advancing toward attacking player (position B), goalie cuts down target area.

line. They drift to the right or left, depending on where the ball is.

But there are times he must leave the goal and advance toward an attacking forward. When he goes out to meet an attacker, he immediately reduces the man's target area (see diagram). And from this position the goalkeeper only has to deflect the ball to the right or left to send it wide of the goal. It sounds easy—but knowing when and how to advance requires a sixth sense that can take years to develop.

SOME OF THE BEST

Generally speaking, there are four types of soccer players in the North American Soccer League. They are classified as forwards, defenders, midfielders, and goalkeepers.

The forwards, also called strikers, are the attacking players. The outside forwards are known as wings or wingers.

The defenders, frequently called backs, concentrate on defense.

The midfielders, sometimes referred to as linkmen, range in between the forwards and defenders.

As for a team's goalkeeper, everyone knows what he does, or is supposed to do.

Most NASL teams use a formation that involves four defenders, three midfielders, and three forwards. Another formation uses four defenders, two midfielders, and four forwards.

During the 1930s, a numbering system was introduced in international soccer, in which each player wore a number that corresponded to the position he played. A goalkeeper wore No. 1. The right back wore No. 2; the left back, No. 3; the right half, No. 4; the center half, No. 5; the left half, No. 6; and so on. If a player who was normally a right back was assigned to play the left back position, he had to switch numbers, from No. 2 to No. 3.

While your favorite goalie may happen to wear No. 1, and while you may see some other players

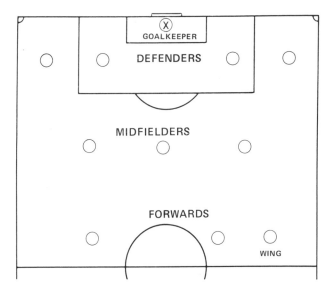

whose numbers correspond to those of the international system, it's more a coincidence than anything else. Americans have cast aside the idea that each number must represent a position. In the NASL, a player is assigned a number when he joins a team, and he wears that number for all time, no matter which position he happens to play.

While each of the various positions on a team requires a different set of skills, there is one characteristic common to every professional player, and that is good physical condition. Teams begin training about six weeks before the season opens, with many clubs now using warm weather locations in the Southeast and Southwest, just as the professional baseball teams have been doing for decades.

But a soccer training camp bears little resemblance to a baseball camp. Baseball players may do 15 or 20 minutes of calisthenics and then spend the rest of their time taking part in batting and fielding drills. There's a great deal of standing around and talking and joking.

But soccer players really work, with much of what they do meant to build their stamina. They perform stretching exercises to get their muscles in shape. They take part in sprinting drills, running to exhaustion. They work to sharpen their skills in shooting, passing, trapping, and heading. Most training sessions conclude with a heated scrimmage.

Soccer players are among the best conditioned of all professional athletes. Each year the ABC television network holds its "Superstars" competition in which professional athletes from all sports compete in a wide range of contests, everything from running and rowboating to bowling and bicycling. It is more than a coincidence that in four of the first five years of competition, a NASL player won. Kyle Rote, Jr., a forward for the Dallas Tornado, was the winner in 1974, 1976, and 1977. Brian Budd, then a forward for the Caribous of Colorado, won in 1978. All that conditioning paid off.

Being in good shape is essential, of course, because soccer players have to be able to run all day. Those that play the forward position not only have to be able to run forever, they have to be able to run fast, too. And the position not only requires speed in the open field, but the ability to explode away from a standing start.

Being fast is particularly important for the forwards who play the wing positions. They often have to be able to beat the players who are covering them on the basis of speed and speed alone.

Forwards must also be exceptionally skilled in ball control, particularly in screening the ball, that is, in using the body to protect the ball from an opposing player. This requires good balance, plus an instinctive awareness of the whereabouts of one's opponent. A forward also has to be an accurate passer.

Those forwards who play the wing positions have to be particularly skilled in dribbling and chipping the ball. A chip pass is normally executed from near the touchline toward the center of the field or even right at the goal mouth. It can be a lob or a hard line drive. Whatever its character, it is very much of a specialty.

When it comes to being nimble-footed, no other forward is quite the equal of Steve David of the California Surf, who often uses his speed to zip right by opposing players. "He makes defenders look like they're walking," his coach once said of him. "He has great quickness, too. He can push the ball forward and get it back before a defender can touch it."

Soccer speedster Steve David

David, a winger, naturally, joined the NASL as a member of the now defunct Miami Toros in 1974. Born in Point Fortin, Trinidad, in 1950, he is 6 feet tall and weighs 155 pounds, the kind of statistics one usually associates with a sprinter. He reportedly can run 100 yards in 9.4, the kind of *time* one usually associates with a sprinter. When he first arrived in Miami, several colleges in the area offered him track scholarships.

During the season of 1975, in a game that the Toros won, 8-0, David scored five goals, a league record. (The record was tied by Giorgio Chinaglia in 1976.) He ended the season as the league's leading scorer, with 23 goals and 6 assists. He became only the third player in NASL history to average more than one goal per game for the season. (He played in 21 games.)

David's importance to the Toros won him the league's Most Valuable Player award in 1975. Pelé was second in balloting.

After the Toros folded, David signed with the Los Angeles Aztecs. There he continued to dazzle opponents—*out*dazzle them, actually—and in 1977 was again the league's top scorer, this time with 26 goals. If it had not been for a late season injury, David might have broken the league's season scoring record of 30 goals. He was named the NASL's Forward of the Year that season. David was traded to Detroit and then to California during 1978.

Left: Chinaglia soars high in an effort to head the ball.

Below: David left Aztecs for Detroit Express during season of 1978.

Those forwards who play in the middle are usually more powerful than the wingers. They have to be able to shoot—really blast the ball—equally well with either foot. Their strength is also important for all of the heading they must do.

If there is one player in the NASL who typifies a forward of this type it is Giorgio Chinaglia (pronounced keen-Al-ya) of the Cosmos. He is big for a forward—6-foot-1, 190 pounds. In fact, he looks more like a football linebacker. Sheer power is what Chinaglia relies upon, not speed or fancy footwork.

A superstar in Italy, where he led Lazio to the Italian first division championship, Chinaglia signed with the Cosmos in time for the 1976 season. He was twenty-nine. As a Cosmos rookie, he scored 19 goals in 19 games to win the NASL scoring title. The next season, after recovering from an early season slump, he registered 15 goals.

Chinaglia, who is married to an American girl and owns a home in Englewood, New Jersey, spends a great deal of time trying to boost American soccer and he is eager to draw more American players into the NASL. But he believes American colleges are inadequate as a training ground. "The colleges play only two or three months a year," he says. "But what do they do the other nine months? I can't see why they don't allow a kid to go to college during the year and also play professional soccer in the summer.

"The colleges don't want this, but time will change them," he predicts.

After Cosmas win, Chinaglia has a wide smile.

With Chinaglia, the Cosmos are blessed with the finest forwards in the game, if not *the* finest. The team can also boast one of the game's premiere midfielders in Franz Beckenbauer, voted the NASL's

Most Valuable Player award in 1977, his first year with the team.

Midfielders, since they both attack and defend, must have the ability to do everything that forwards and backs do. But if there is one quality that a midfielder must have above all others, it is the ability to run constantly and never tire. They're always on the move.

Traditionally, the best midfielders have been small and aggressive players. Being small isn't necessary, but being aggressive is. Aggressiveness is what's needed to tackle and win the ball. Midfielders also have to be intelligent and accurate with their passes, for they frequently can trigger scoring opportunities for their team.

Not only is Beckenbauer an outstanding midfielder, he is an unusual one. He has exceptional ball control skills, and sometimes dribbles with all the wizardry of a winger. He also has excellent balance and the ability to change pace deceptively. He's extremely quick at getting off the mark.

When on defense, Beckenbauer sometimes shows up far downfield, a trait that can be traced to the days when he played sweeper. A sweeper is a defensive player who is stationed in front of the goalkeeper. Should someone slip through the defense, the sweeper picks him up.

Beckenbauer played the position of sweeper like no one before him. Instead of merely serving as a defensive fail-safe, pouncing on any attacking player

As hero of German soccer, Beckenbauer was the idol of millions.

who cracked through the defenses, Beckenbauer, with his unrivaled sense of strategy, would take the ball and trigger a scoring drive. In this respect he was frequently compared to ice hockey's Bobby Orr, the Boston Bruin defenseman of the recent past who had the speed and power to generate scoring thrusts from his defenseman's post.

Beckenbauer was a sweeper for six years in Germany and played the position in his first days with the Cosmos. But when coach Eddie Firmani took over the team during the 1977 season, he switched Beckenbauer to midfield where he believed that better use could be made of his skills.

At the time he signed with the Cosmos, Beckenbauer ranked as Europe's most highly regarded player. As captain of West Germany's Bayern Munchen club, he led the team to three European Cups and, in 1974, to a World Cup title.

Although he is known primarily as a defensive player, as a youngster he achieved fame as a scorer.

"Once, when I was fourteen," he has recalled, "we beat a team, 25-0. I scored 17 goals."

His great potential was well known throughout Germany. Kurt Lamm, secretary of the United States Soccer Federation, once recalled visiting the noted German coach Sepp Herberger, who had files

For Cosmos, Beckenbauer directs operations from midfield post.

Aztecs' George Best ranks as one of game's most instinctive players.

on every European soccer player. Lamm took out Beckenbauer's card from the file and read it. It said: "Can be a great player, perhaps the greatest ever."

Beckenbauer first caught the public's eye in 1966 when he played for West Germany's World Cup team. Although only twenty then, he displayed rare intelligence, artistry, and coolness.

No player is more serious about soccer than Beckenbauer. When he left Germany for the United States to join the Cosmos, he took sixteen pairs of soccer shoes with him. On the first day that he stepped out onto the Astroturf of Giants Stadium where the Cosmos play their home games, Beckenbauer was wearing exactly the right type of shoes for that surface.

The explosive George Best of the Ft. Lauderdale Strikers plays the midfield position in more of a classic manner than Beckenbauer. Wonderfully instinctive, he is noted for his ability to send "blind" passes to his cutting wings. He had 18 assists and scored 11 goals himself in 1977 as a member of the Los Angeles Aztecs, and was named Midfielder of the Year.

Best is well-known for his flamboyant off-the-field conduct. Even on the field he can be unorthodox. Once, in the days he played for Manchester United, Best was being closely and roughly guarded by Ron Harris, a player who was known as "Chopper" for his aggressive play. After he had taken almost an entire half of punishment, Best, holding one foot

Defensive star Mike Connell

on the ball, pulled off his red shirt, and waved it at Harris as if it were a bullfighter's cape, taunting him to come and try to take the ball away.

The type of bizarre conduct which Best sometimes displays would never be indulged in by a defensive player. A defender has to be, first and foremost, a strong tackler, a sure tackler. This not only requires physical strength, but also a hostile attitude. There's no funny business about playing defense. "You have to *want* to go and get the ball," says one coach. "You have to be something of a brawler. If you don't like to mix it up, you can't expect to do well."

These words pretty much describe Mike Connell of the Tampa Bay Rowdies. "He's a tenacious player," says a spokesman for the team. "He's got a never-say-die attitude."

Only eighteen when he joined the Rowdies in 1975, Connell is a native of Johannesburg, South Africa. He played every minute of every game in his first two seasons with the team.

Connell admits that his aggressiveness has played a part in his success. "Right at the start of a game," he says, "you have to make the forwards know you're there, do something to make them remember you. Otherwise, they'll walk all over you."

Of course, there are other skills involved. "Every opposing player in the vicinity of the goal must be in your eyesight," says Connell. "And when one of those men plays the ball, you must make him play it *away* from the goal."

Mike England (left) and Mel Machin, All-Star defenders for the Seattle Sounders

How important is defense? Well, a strong defense is what propelled the Seattle Sounders into the Soccer Bowl in 1977. Their defenders that year included not only Rookie of the Year Jim McAlister, but two members of the league's All-Star team, Mike England, a tall and rangy Welshman, and Mel Machin, who not only was skilled in keeping the ball away from the Sounders' goal, but added offensive strength with his accurate crossing passes.

As Jim McAlister has clearly demonstrated, American players often excel as defenders, more so than as forwards. This is undoubtedly because the position does not demand quite so much ball control ability. Americans have also done well as goalkeepers. Bronx-born Shep Messing of the Oakland Stompers is one example.

Messing is an acrobat in the net, catapulting from one post to the other. Or he will come bounding out of the goal toward an attacker, screaming at him as he runs, and then at the last second, he will fling his body at the ball.

"I don't believe in playing a defensive goal," Messing says. "I'm aggressive. I like to make forwards think twice when they come into my area."

In his will to win, Messing sometimes goes beyond what is right and honorable. Once, in a game in Boston, Messing noticed that the goal in which he was to work had movable posts. The referee checked the posts just before the game began to be sure they were the right distance apart. "But as soon as he

"I don't believe in playing a defensive goal," says Shep Messing.

95

Gordon Banks has been called the best goalkeeper in the world.

turned away, I moved the posts six inches closer," Messing says. "Of course, at the end of the half, I had to remember to open them up again so we'd have all the room we were supposed to have to shoot at."

Other outstanding American goalkeepers have included Arnie Mausser of the Tampa Bay Rowdies and Bob Rigby of the Aztecs. Mausser, who had an excellent goals-per-game average of 1.17 in 1976, is from Brooklyn. Bob Rigby, the NASL's leading goalkeeper in 1973, and, after Kyle Rote, the game's most popular player that year, was born in Ridley Park, Pennsylvania.

What's the explanation? Why is it that Americans can outshine foreign-born players as goalkeepers? The answer is easy. Most American ball games are hand-oriented, and goalkeeping is a position in which sure hands are vital.

If, however, one had to choose the best goalkeeper of recent years, an Englishman, Gordon Banks of the Ft. Lauderdale Strikers, would undoubtedly get the designation. Indeed, Banks has been rated by many as the best goalkeeper in the world.

He certainly was that in 1966 and 1970, the years he served as goalkeeper on England's World Cup teams. He was England's Footballer of the Year in 1972.

Pelé once paid Banks an extraordinary tribute. It was triggered by a play Banks made in a first round game of the 1970 World Cup in Guadalajara, Mexico, with Péle's Brazilian team matched against Banks' English team. A Brazilian player, Jairzinho, sped down the right side, and sent a high crossing pass to Pelé, who leapt into the air to line a header for the far corner of the goal.

Banks, from the middle of the goal, sprang toward the corner. He saw the ball bounce just short of the goal line and made up his mind where it was going to go. Pelé, certain he had scored, was beginning to thrust his arms over his head in triumph. But then he saw Banks' outstretched right hand reaching out and just tip the ball over the net. "It was the greatest save I have ever seen by the greatest goalie I have ever played against," Pelé said afterward.

In 1973, Banks was touched by tragedy. A car he was driving smashed head-on into a van. He was pulled unconscious from the wreckage, his face so torn that it required 108 stitches. Worse, he lost the sight of his right eye.

When he tried playing goalkeeper again, Banks was sad to watch. He seemed uncertain, and in lunging for balls often went too high or too low. Doctors said he had lost much of his depth perception.

When Ron Newman took over as head coach of the Strikers in 1977, he asked Banks to come out of retirement and try his hand in the goal once more. "I thought that Banks could be a top goalkeeper in the NASL," Newman says. "I thought that when you

The agile Banks leaps for high one during Striker warm-up drill.

become the world's best at anything, you have the character and willingness to work hard to try to be the best again."

What happened is one of the most warming stories in recent sports history. Once he had whipped his body into shape, Banks put on one superb performance after another, ending up with a goals-against average of 1.12, which made him the second stingiest goalie in the league. He also posted nine shutouts, second best in the league, and in the All-Star balloting, Banks captured more votes than any other player, more even than Pelé or Beckenbauer.

Early in 1978, the Strikers played several exhibition games in England. Fans there hadn't forgotten Banks and his World Cup performances, and mobbed him after every game. Police had to be called to help get him off the field. If Banks' career goes on much longer, scenes like that are sure to be duplicated at Lockhart Stadium in Ft. Lauderdale.

Pile-ups like this one were common in soccer's early days, when dribbling was the chief offensive weapon.

THE TACTICAL GAME

In its early years, soccer was much more a game of individuals than a team game. The player who had possession of the ball dribbled it until he lost it. Passing came later.

With passing came formations, various systems for aligning the players. Most NASL teams use the 4-3-3 system today, which incorporates a goalkeeper, four defenders, three midfielders, and three forwards. (In soccer formations, the first number tells how many players are back on defense; the second number, how many have midfield responsibilities; and the third, how many attackers there are. The goalkeeper is never included, since his position never changes.)

The fact that soccer teams are deployed in formations should not imply that you can look out on the field and expect to see the players moving in neat rows. A formation is never static. Players are not bound by hard-and-fast rules. There has to be individual freedom; there has to be constant movement.

Indeed, if there is one quality that professionals have that separates them from amateurs, it is the ability to be able to anticipate what is going to be happening and react accordingly. The professional thinks ahead. He moves on the basis of where the ball is going to be, not on the basis of where it happens to be at any given moment.

Even the player designations—forward, midfielder, and defender—can be misleading. A defender can attack; a forward can help out on defense.

During soccer's formative years, that is, during the period when the tactical game was based on dribbling and dribbling alone, there was no need to align players in formations. The man who had the ball would dribble past as many opponents as he could. When he lost the ball to an opposing player, that man would then dribble until *he* lost it.

A team was composed of a goalkeeper, one full-back, two halfbacks, and seven forwards. But positions didn't mean much. Everyone followed the ball around.

A tactical advance came in the 1870s when it was suggested that when a player was in possession of the ball and dribbling, a teammate might follow his path, keeping alert to recover the ball when the dribbler came under attack. "Backing up," the strategy was called.

A more profound change came in 1872. Scotland played England in an international match in Glasgow. When the English players returned home, they told of a new system of "combination" play that the Scots had used. It was based on short passes made along the ground.

The concept of passing the ball changed the game drastically. No longer was it wise for players to bunch together around the ball. Now they spread out, with teams covering the entire field.

The era of positional play was dawning. Through a process of trial and error that followed the introduction of the short pass, the first of soccer's classic formations evolved—the 2-3-5. Also known as the pyramid, it was made up of two defenders, three midfielders, and five forwards.

The 2-3-5 stood as the dominant formation for the next fifty years. During this time, the long pass was introduced. This changed the game, too. Since the ball was in the air more, added emphasis had to be placed on trapping and heading.

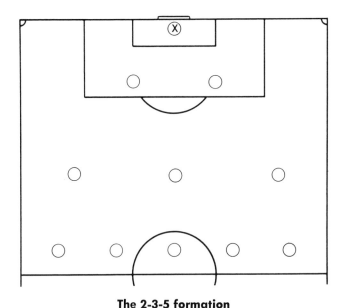

The 2-3-5 formation

A change in the rules triggered the next tactical innovations. Soccer experienced a period of dullness during the 1920s. The offside rule then in effect was the reason. It stated that an attacking player had to have at least *three* opponents between himself and the goal as he received the ball. If there were not three defenders in front of him, play was halted and the defending team was awarded a free kick.

Clever defenders exploited this rule. When a team was under attack, one of the two fullbacks, instead of falling back to defend the goal, would race up field, leaving only the other forward and the goalkeeper deep. One of the opposing forwards couldn't help but be guilty of an offside violation.

The number of goals being scored was dwindling because the "offside trap," as the maneuver was called, was being used so frequently. Spectators complained loudly.

In 1925, the offside rule was changed. The revised version stated that an offside player had to have only two opponents between himself and the goal. In order to exploit this rule, both fullbacks would have to race upfield, leaving the goalkeeper on his own.

Now the balance of power swung in the other direction, toward the offense. Forwards, free to move as they wished, were responsible for a dramatic increase in the number of goals scored.

The famous Arsenal club of North London was the first to react tactically to what was happening. The Arsenal manager and captain decided that the two fullbacks incorporated in the 2-3-5 system were no longer sufficient. Three fullbacks were what was needed.

Arsenal made their center their third fullback. To compensate for the weakness this move created in the midfield area, the two inside forwards were drawn back toward the center of the field. If you had gotten aboard a helicopter and hovered above a team aligned in this fashion, it would look as if the players were spelling out a giant W atop a giant M

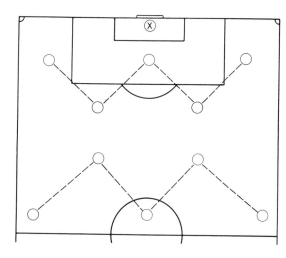

The W-M formation

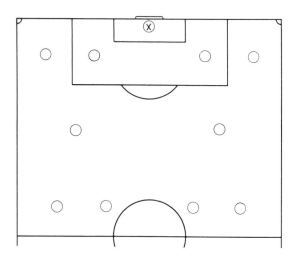

The 4-2-4 formation

(see diagram). The W-M formation is what it was called.

The W-M formation lasted from the mid-1920s to the 1950s, the period when Hungary and Brazil began producing winning teams that employed four defenders in a line across the field, a four-man attacking line, and two linkmen—a 4-2-4 formation. When the Brazilians won the World Cup in 1958, their team used the 4-2-4.

Despite all those backs, the 4-2-4 was a strong offensive formation. As played by the Brazilians, the outside fullbacks were instructed to move upfield as far as the center line when their team was on the attack. Thus, as many as eight players could be involved in an offensive thrust.

While the 4-2-4 could be adapted to give a numerical advantage on the attack, it also provided for a strong defensive framework. In the Brazilian scheme of things, the left wing was frequently withdrawn toward the goal, acting as a third midfielder.

When the Brazilians captured the World Cup four years later, in 1962, they had withdrawn their left wing on a permanent basis. In other words, the 4-2-4 had become the 4-3-3 formation.

Meanwhile, another tactical development had been taking place in Italy. This put the emphasis, not on any offensive strategy, but upon wrecking

102

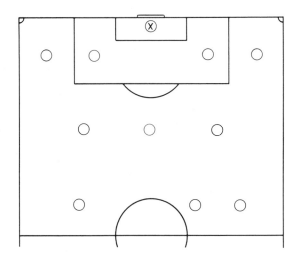

The 4-3-3 formation

the other team's offense; it emphasized defense.

In 1947, Triestina, a small Italian club, in an effort to avoid being dominated by the bigger, more powerful clubs, began to position a fullback behind the three defensive backs, with the man assigned to cover the area immediately in front of the ball. This man was known as a *libero*, or free man. Later, when English teams adopted the *libero* principle, they called the man a "sweeper."

Triestina and the other small Italian clubs had remarkable success with their new defensive system, which became known as the *catenaccio* system. *Catenaccio* means "big chain." It was so-called because of the chainlike barrier of defenders it put across the field.

The *catenaccio* system could be made even more difficult to deal with by putting the *libero* behind a line of four fullbacks, instead of three. In the hands of diligent and determined defenders, the *catenaccio* made it almost impossible to score. Eventually, Italy's biggest club adopted one variation or another of the *catenaccio* defense.

When Brazil met Italy in the World Cup final in 1970, the Brazilians used a mixture of the 4-3-3 and the 4-2-4 formations. The Italians were defense-minded, relying on the *catenaccio*. Brazil carried the day, overwhelming the Italians by a score of 4-1. But it was not their tactical skill that made the

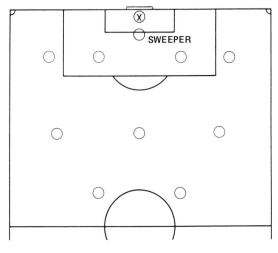

The *catenaccio*

For his ability as a goal scorer, German fans called Gerd Muller "Der Bomber."

Brazilians great. It was their spirit and fluidity, and the fact that the Brazilian players were offense-minded, rather than stressing the negativism that the *catenaccio* implied.

West Germany won the World Cup in 1974. Two years before, the West Germans had won the European Nations Cup, which is regarded as being as important as the World Cup in Europe. Like the Brazilian World Cup champions of 1970, the West Germans played a spirited, freewheeling brand of soccer. And in Gerd Muller, the team boasted the most prolific scorer in international soccer. Muller slammed in goals with his head, chest, or either foot. German fans called him "Der Bomber."

In the final Cup match in 1974, the Germans faced Holland. The favored Dutch scored a quick goal. But after that, the Dutch team could never get its attack working smoothly again, and the Germans went on to win by a 2-1 score.

When the Dutch attack was clicking, it was something to see. Called "the Dutch whirl," many observers felt that it represented a significant step forward in international soccer. Constant movement was the keynote of the system, with all ten players appearing to play any position on the field, with any man attacking when the opportunity was there.

The Dutch whirl was the 4-3-3, 4-2-4, 2-3-5, and 4-4-2 all rolled into one. It was none of these, yet it has elements of them all. One could no more diagram the Dutch whirl than one could diagram a game of playground tag.

Of all the Dutch players, Johan Cruyff was the most creative and deceptive. He could jerk his leg one way, convincing defenders he was launching a powerful kick, but then he would lift his foot over the ball and tap it backward. He was quick and fast. He dribbled the ball so that it looked, according to one observer, "as if it were tied to his foot with a string."

Hopefully, Johan Cruyff and his orange-shirted Dutch teammates freed international soccer from the restraints of the *catenaccio* and other defense-minded systems. More individuality and flexibility mean more exciting soccer for the fan.

The tactical systems in use in the NASL today—the 4-3-3 and 4-2-4—provide the framework for whatever strategy a team wishes to use at any given time. The midfield X is one such piece of strategy. When a team in possession of the ball approaches the critical midfield area, it often relies on the X to outwit the defense and keep the ball moving.

Imagine the outside halfbacks and the inside

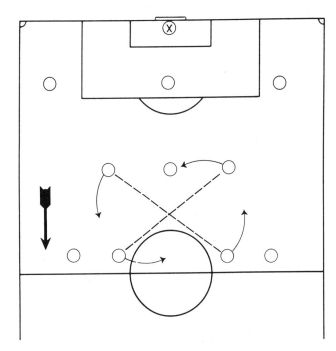

The midfield X

forwards to be at each of the four corners of an X. As they advance, they switch positions while keeping possession of the ball. For example, the right half will dribble from the bottom left-hand corner of the X to the top left-hand corner. As he does so, his three teammates rotate in a counterclockwise direction. The X has remained intact, but the players are in different positions.

When the half reaches the top of the X, he passes the ball diagonally back, that is, to the bottom

When a team works the ball close to the opposition goal, the defense tightens. Here Cosmos Giorgio Chinaglia finds, not one, but two players obstructing his path to the ball.

right-hand corner of the X. The receiver dribbles to the top of the X and the players rotate in the opposite direction. Now the strategy is ready to be repeated.

When a team has advanced the ball to a position near the goal, it's often wise to pass to a player close to one of the sidelines. Doing so causes the defense to shift to that side, a piece of strategy that is known as "turning the defense." Once the defense has been turned, the player in possession often attempts to pass to a teammate on the far side of the field who has slipped into the area vacated by the defensive players.

Defensive systems that teams use are less complex. Some teams employ a man-to-man play, each defending player covering a particular member of the offensive team. For example, the two fullbacks mark the wings. The center half covers the center forward, and the two halfbacks guard the inside forwards.

In a zone defense, each player is assigned to cover a specific area of the field. Sometimes a team will use a man-to-man defense as the attacking team advances, but switch to a zone when play gets close to the goal they're defending. The zone defense is surer. A defensive player can't be lured out of position, thereby leaving a portion of the field undefended, a failing of any man-to-man system.

The closer the ball gets to the goal, the smaller the zones of coverage become. Also, they must

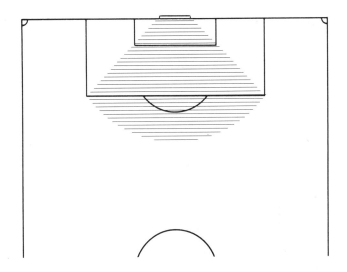

Shaded area indicates danger zone for defense.

overlap; otherwise, an attacking player could filter through the "seam" where two zones meet, and break for the goal.

When a team is on defense, it may permit the opposition to penetrate to midfield and even beyond, the defensive players retreating as the ball is advanced. The defensive team will even concede space beyond the midfield line and on the flanks of the penalty area. But the area that extends outward from the goal toward the corners of the penalty area is regarded as a danger zone by the defense. The real test for the offensive team is whether it can penetrate that zone.

WHAT DOES A COACH DO?

During a basketball game, the coach never stops working, planning strategy with his assistants, signaling for time-outs, making lineup changes, shouting encouragement to the men on the floor, and occasionally arguing with the referee.

The coach in football is even more involved, some to the extent that they call each play the quarterback runs, sending in "messenger" substitutes with their instructions.

But what does a soccer coach do during a game? The rules limit substitutions. Only three are permitted during an entire game, so there's not much to do in that department.

And a soccer coach can't call a time-out to plan strategy. In soccer, there are no time-outs.

What does a soccer coach do besides pace up and down in front of the bench and chew his fingernails?

Take, for example, Ron Newman, head coach of the Ft. Lauderdale Strikers, one of the most successful of all pro soccer coaches during the decade of the 1970s. From England, the affable Newman played professional soccer there from 1954 through 1966, and in 1967 signed a contract with the Atlanta Chiefs of the NASL. The following year he became an assistant coach with the Dallas Tornado, and in 1969 he took over as head coach, a post he held through 1975.

The team he inherited in Dallas was in pitiful shape, having won only two of 32 games the previous season, a league record for futility. Newman completely reconstructed the team and, in 1971, captured the NASL championship. In the three years that followed, Dallas won two more division titles and never failed to gain a playoff berth.

After the 1975 season, Newman left Dallas to join the newly organized Los Angeles Skyhawks of the American Soccer League. He promptly led that team to the league championship, losing only two games and winning honors as the ASL's Coach of the Year. Newman thus ranks as the first and only coach to win championships in both professional leagues.

In 1977, Newman was back in the NASL as head coach of the Strikers, a team which had played as the Miami Toros the year before and had finished dead last in the Eastern Division of the Atlantic Conference. Because of their dismal showing the previous season, the Strikers loomed as an also-ran, but not to Newman. "I had players who didn't want to join the club because they didn't think we had a chance for the title," he recalls. "I told them, 'You don't know me; I've always had competitive teams.'"

Newman demonstrated his magic once more, finishing with the best won-lost percentage in the league and the Eastern Division championship. The Strikers' 19 regular season victories equaled the

Just before kickoff, Newman has final instructions for Colin Fowles (center) and Curtis Leeper. "Concentrate out there," he told them. "You *must* concentrate."

NASL's season record and were a principal reason Newman captured Coach of the Year honors by a landslide margin.

The first thing that Newman does in preparing his team for a game is to evaluate the strengths and weaknesses of the opposition. He speculates on how each of the Striker players are going to adapt to the opposing players and the tactics those players are going to be using. "I think about the game day and night," Newman says. "I keep playing it over and over in my head."

Out of this brainwork, Newman develops his

Newman watches Strikers stoically.

lineup for the game, choosing players who he feels will be the most effective against the opposition, benching those who may be lacking in some way. "Maybe the opposition has an attacking forward who is very fast, and the man who would ordinarily be covering him doesn't like speed. That means I have to make an adjustment there." He makes similar judgments for each position on the team.

Newman also catalogs the opposition's strong points. "Maybe they're a team that's particularly strong on corner kicks," he says. "They have a man who can curve the ball skillfully. Maybe they're very good on free kicks. I'll warn my players about these things and tell them to be ready."

In American professional football, teams assign scouts to watch an upcoming opponent and develop a detailed analysis of the enemy. Game films of the opponent are carefully studied. From the scouting reports and the films, a detailed "game plan" is prepared. Each member of the team receives a copy. It sets down the role each man is to play.

These concepts are not followed in pro soccer. "I would never use film of an opponent in preparing my team for a game," Ron Newman says. "Films can give a wrong impression. By watching an opposition forward outshoot a goalie or consistently outrace opposing defenders, my players might get the idea that the man is invincible. It's easier for a man to defend against an opponent than the film suggests."

Nor does Newman give detailed assignments to his players. Instead, he keeps things general. "Watch this man when he cuts," he'll tell a player. "Be careful when this man drops back," he'll say to another.

"You can't fill up players' heads with information," Newman says. "You don't want them to have too much on their minds. Soccer is a game of thinking, a game of concentration. Each man has to be able to react in a split second to any one of a number of game situations. A man can't react if you clutter his brain with a lot of facts and figures."

In other words, Newman recognizes soccer as a sport in which the players must act creatively. "You can't be a robot," he says.

Yet Newman recognizes the value of preparing the team psychologically for a game. "When I address the players before they go out onto the field, I try to stress why this particular game is important," he says. "Maybe it's important to us as far as the league standings are concerned. Perhaps the team is one of our chief rivals, such as the Cosmos are. Or maybe there's a player on the opposition team who's been particularly troublesome to us.

"I also try to speak to individual players before they go out onto the field. I'll tell a player what I'm expecting of him, maybe give him a few words of encouragement, and clap him on the back."

What Newman does not do is try to get the team

Following a Striker win, Newman takes part in postgame interview.

into a "ready-to-kill" frame of mind. "I want the players at a psychological and physical peak," he says. "I want them eager to play. But I don't want them charging out onto the field like a bunch of maniacs. If they do that, they won't be able to think; they won't be able to concentrate. I want them cool, so they can use their heads."

Once the game begins, what does Newman do? "Mostly," he told me, "I sit and worry."

That's not quite true. At the kickoff, Newman dons horned-rim glasses and takes up a position behind the bench where he *stands* and worries. A vein throbs in his lower jaw as he stares out at the action, his expression hardly changing.

Throughout the game, he shouts encouragement and instructions.

"*This* way! *This* way!" he yells to a player who is dribbling by.

"Tsk, tsk, tsk," he utters when the player fails to follow his advice and loses the ball.

"Nico, Nico," he calls out sadly to forward Nico Bodonczy, saying to him, "That's the only place he *could* go."

"Put it down!" he shouts to a player who sends a high pass to a teammate.

"*Don't* run past him!" he shouts to another man who has gotten dangerously out of position.

"No one's over there!" he says in horror at the sight of a misdirected pass.

Newman has words for the officials, too. "Hey, ref," he shouts. "Watch the linesman."

Another time, when the referee's whistle sounds, halting a Striker scoring thrust, Newman shakes his head in disgust and says, "How can you stop the bloody game like that?"

When the first half is over and the players file into the locker room, Newman talks to them again, telling them what they've been doing right and what they've been doing wrong. He may make some changes in the lineup. He may adjust the positioning of some of the players. Or he may not make any changes at all. "From a tactical standpoint," Newman says, "what a soccer team is supposed to do is create scoring chances for itself, while denying scoring chances to the opposition. If we're doing both of these things, I won't make any changes, even if

Newman trades grins with coach Eddie Firmani before game against Cosmos.

113

Thrashing by Cosmos put a scowl on Newman's face.

we happen to be trailing. I know we'll come out on top at the end—or at least we *should* come out on top."

During the second half, Newman is watchful for players who fail to concentrate on their assignments. "Concentration is vital to success," Newman says. "If a player doesn't concentrate, he can't do his job."

When players begin to get fatigued, their concentration can dissolve. Or the crowd, by cheering a player or booing him, can distract him.

"C'mon, Alan!" Newman shouts. "C'mon, Nico!" A player hearing his name knows that he hasn't been doing what he's supposed to have been doing. "I try to bring them back to life," says Newman.

Of course, what Newman does during a game represents only one aspect of his job. He spends a minimum of two-and-one-half months getting the team ready for the season. In 1978, the Strikers made a nineteen-day training trip to England during February. There they played several English football (it's not called soccer in England) teams.

When the Strikers returned to the United States, they began daily workouts in Ft. Lauderdale, with the drills meant to improve players' skills and build their endurance. Players from foreign countries also have to get used to the way the ball behaves in Florida. "The grass and atmosphere are different and they affect the ball's flight," says Newman, "the way it bounces, and the way it bends in the air."

It's Newman who conducts the team's practice sessions. It's Newman who must evaluate the players and make the decisions as to which ones are to be retained and which are to be released.

Newman makes the Strikers' selections during the NASL draft sessions in New York each winter. Newman is the principal speaker at the "Meet the Strikers Breakfast" held in Ft. Lauderdale just before the season opens. He helps officiate at the annual beauty contest to select the young women who serve as hostesses at the team's home games. (They're called "Striker Psychers.")

Newman has a hundred-and-one different duties and responsibilities. But when a game is being played, the rules of soccer put a limit on what he can do. The outcome rests with the players and how well Newman has prepared them. "Worrying is about all I can do," he says. "It's very frustrating."

GLOSSARY

AMERICAN SOCCER LEAGUE (ASL)—An organization of professional soccer clubs representing approximately a dozen American cities.

BACK—A defender.

BREAKAWAY—A game situation in which a player in possession of the ball eludes the last defending player and bears in on the goal.

CATENACCIO—A formation that uses two strikers, three midfielders, and four defenders in the defensive half of the field, plus a sweeper in front of the goalkeeper.

CENTER CIRCLE—A circle in the center of the field having a radius of 10 yards with the center spot. Also called the kickoff circle.

CENTER SPOT—A spot at the very center of the field upon which the ball is spotted for kickoffs.

CLEAR—A kick by the goalkeeper that sends the ball far downfield, away from the goal; also, a pass by a defender with the same purpose.

CORNER AREA—A quarter-circle with a 1-yard radius drawn inside the playing field at each corner. The ball is placed within the corner area for a corner kick.

CORNER KICK—A free kick awarded the attacking team from a corner area after a defending player has driven the ball beyond his own goal line.

CROSS—A long pass by a wing toward a teammate nearing the goal, within the penalty area.

DEFENDER—A player whose job it is to prevent the opposition from penetrating and who assists the goal-keeper in protecting the goal.

DIRECT FREE KICK—A free kick awarded a team when an opposing player commits a foul such as holding, tripping, or kicking. A goal may be scored directly from a direct free kick.

DRIBBLE—To advance the ball by tapping it with either foot.

FEDERATION INTERNATIONALE DE FOOTBALL ASSOCIATION (FIFA)—The governing body of soccer throughout the world. With headquarters in Zurich, Switzerland, FIFA has a membership of more than 140 nations.

FORWARD—A member of the attacking line whose job it is to score goals or help create scoring opportunities.

FOUL—A violation of the rules which is penalized by awarding a direct free kick or an indirect free kick to the opposing team.

FREE KICK—A kick of a stationary ball awarded one team for a rule infraction by the other. There are two types: the direct free kick and indirect free kick.

FULLBACK—A primarily defensive player.

GOAL—The structure into which the ball must be played for a score. It is 8 feet high and 8 yards wide and backed by a net.

GOAL AREA—The rectangular area in front of each goal that measures 6 yards by 20 yards. Goal kicks are taken from within the goal area.

GOALKEEPER—The player who is stationed in front of the goal and serves as a team's last line of defense. The goalkeeper is the only player permitted to play the ball with his hands (but he may do so only within the penalty area).

GOAL KICK—An indirect free kick given a defensive player when the ball has been driven out of bounds over the goal line by an attacking player. The kick is taken from within the goal area and must clear the penalty area.

GOAL LINE—The boundary line at either end of the field. A ball driven over the goal line but not into the goal is out of bounds.

GOAL MOUTH—The area immediately in front of the goal.

HALF VOLLEY—To kick the ball just as it rebounds from the ground.

HEADING—Using one's head to pass, shoot, or control the ball.

INDIRECT FREE KICK—A free kick awarded a team when a member of the opposing team commits a foul such as obstructing an opponent, charging the goalkeeper, or dangerous play. Being offside also results in an indirect free kick. A goal cannot be scored directly from an indirect free kick.

KICKOFF—The method of starting play at the beginning of a half or following a goal in which a stationary ball is kicked from the center spot to a teammate of the kicker.

KICKOFF CIRCLE—See Center circle.

LIBERO—See Sweeper.

LINESMAN—One of two officials who works along a touchline, assisting the referee by indicating when a ball or player has gone out of bounds.

LINKMAN—A midfielder.

LOB—A high and arcing kick that travels over the heads of the opponents.

MARK—To guard an opponent.

MIDFIELDER—One of the players who is stationed between the forwards and defenders.

NORTH AMERICAN SOCCER LEAGUE (NASL)—An organization of professional soccer clubs representing twenty-four American and Canadian cities (as of 1978); soccer's principal professional league.

OFFSIDE—A rule violation that occurs when a player who is receiving a pass in the attacking half of the field permits fewer than two defenders (including the goalkeeper) to be nearer to the goal than he is.

PENALTY ARC—An arc that has a radius of 10 yards with the penalty spot as its center, and which extends beyond the far end of the penalty area.

PENALTY AREA—The rectangular area at each end of the field in front of each goal that measures 18 by 44 yards.

PENALTY KICK—A direct free kick at the goal defended only by the goalkeeper that is awarded an attacking player after being fouled within the penalty area. The ball is placed on the penalty spot. All players on both teams must leave the penalty area and the adjoining arc during the attempt.

PENALTY SPOT—A small circle on the field that is equidistant from the sidelines and 12 yards in front of the goal. The ball is placed on the penalty spot for a penalty kick.

REFEREE—The official who supervises play. He penalizes infractions by awarding free kicks and rules when goals have been scored.

SAVE—A blocked shot by a goalkeeper.

SCREEN—When dribbling, to protect the ball by keeping the body between the ball and the defender.

SHOOT-OUT—The tie-breaking system used in the NASL. When the score is still tied after two overtime periods, each one of five players from each team takes an unopposed shot at the goalkeeper. The team scoring the most goals wins the game.

SOCCER BOWL—Annual competition in the North American Soccer League between the winner of the American Conference and National Conference for the league championship.

STRIKER—An attacking player; a forward.

SWEEPER—A defensive player who is positioned behind the defensive line and in front of the goal. Also called a *libero*.

TACKLE—To use one's feet to take the ball from an opponent.

TRAP—To bring a moving ball under control by stopping or deflecting it.

UNITED STATES SOCCER FEDERATION (USSF)—The governing body of soccer in the United States. Besides providing the standard rules of play, the USSF promotes the game with schools, colleges, and local associations.

VOLLEY—To kick the ball before it touches the ground.

WALL PASS—A pass that is kicked back immediately to the passer (after the passer has gone by the player defending him).

WING; WINGER—The right or left outside forward.

WORLD CUP—Soccer competition held every four years among teams representing nations of the world and which represents world supremacy in soccer.

ALL-TIME NASL RECORDS

INDIVIDUAL RECORDS

Most Goals Scored, Season
34—Giorgio Chinaglia (Cosmos), 1978

Most Goals Scored, Game
5—Ron Moore (Chicago) vs. Vancouver, June 24, 1977; Giorgio Chinaglia (Cosmos) vs. Miami, August 10, 1976; Steve David (Miami) vs. Washington, June 20, 1975

Most Goals Scored, One Half
4—Andy Provan (Philadelphia) vs. Washington, May 4, 1974; Giorgio Chinaglia (Cosmos) vs. Miami, August 10, 1976

Most Consecutive Games Scoring a Goal
10—Steve David (Los Angeles), 1977

Most Goals on Penalty Kicks, Season
8—Keith Eddy (Cosmos), 1976

Most Goals on Penalty Kicks, Game
2—Manfred Eickerling (Boston) vs. Rochester, July 20, 1974

Most Assists, Season
18—George Best (Los Angeles), 1977; Pelé (Cosmos), 1976

Most Assists, Game
4—Vito Dimitijevic (Cosmos) vs. Toronto, June 5, 1977; Roberto Aguirre (Miami) vs. Cosmos, June 14, 1974; Miguel Perrichon (Toronto) vs. Miami, May 6, 1972

Most Assists, One Half
3—Alan Wooler (Boston) vs. Cosmos, August 3, 1975; Roberto Aguirre (Miami) vs. Cosmos, June 14, 1974; Ian Filby (Montreal) vs. Rochester, July 17, 1973; Miguel Perrichon (Toronto) vs. Miami, May 6, 1972

Most Consecutive Games with an Assist
5—George Best (Los Angeles), 1977; Carlos Metidieri (Rochester), 1971

GOALKEEPER RECORDS

Fewest Goals Allowed, Season
8—Bob Rigby (Philadelphia), 1973

Best Goals-against Average, Season
0.62—Bob Rigby (Philadelphia), 1973; Mirko Stojanovic (Dallas), 1971

Most Consecutive Shutouts, Season
4—Zeljko Bilecki (Toronto), 1975; Ken Cooper (Dallas), 1974; Claude Campos (Rochester), 1973, 1974

Most Shutouts, Season
12—Lincoln Phillips (Washington), 1970

Most Consecutive Minutes Without Allowing Goal, One Season
476—Claude Campos (Rochester), 1972

Most Saves, Game
22—Mike Winter (St. Louis) vs. Rochester, May 27, 1973

Most Goals Allowed, Season
52—Peter Fox (Hawaii), 1977

TEAM RECORDS

Most Games Won, Season
24—Cosmos, 1978

Highest Winning Percentage, Season
.800—Cosmos, 1978 (24 of 30)

Fewest Games Won, Season
2—Baltimore, 1969; Dallas, 1968

Lowest Winning Percentage, Season
.062—Dallas, 1968 (2 of 32)

Most Consecutive Games Won
8—Los Angeles, 1974; Oakland, 1968

Most Consecutive Games Without a Loss
14—Dallas, 1974

Most Games Lost, Season
26—Dallas, 1968

Most Consecutive Games Lost
11—Hartford, 1975

Most Consecutive Games Without a Victory
22—Dallas, 1968

Most Goals Scored, Season
71—Oakland, 1968; Cosmos, 1978

Highest Goals Per Game Average, Season
3.3—Kansas City, 1969 (53 goals in 16 games)

Most Goals, Game
9—Cosmos (vs. Washington), June 29, 1975; Oakland (vs. St. Louis), July 26, 1967

Largest Margin of Victory
9—Oakland vs. St. Louis, July 26, 1967 (9-0)

Most Shots, Game
45—Hawaii (vs. Los Angeles), July 22, 1977

Most Shots, Game, Both Teams
66—Baltimore (42) vs. San Jose (24), May 24, 1976; New York (43) vs. Rochester (23), June 9, 1971

Fewest Shots, Game
1—Rochester (vs. Toronto), July 6, 1975

Fewest Shots, Game, Both Teams
16—Vancouver (9) vs. Hartford (7), May 25, 1975; Dallas (9) vs. Toronto (7), May 5, 1973

Most Goals Allowed, Season
109—Dallas, 1968

Highest Average Goals Per Game Allowed, Season
3.4—Dallas, 1968 (109 in 32 games)

Most Goals Allowed, Game
9—St. Louis (vs. Oakland), July 26, 1967; Washington (vs. Cosmos), June 29, 1975

Fewest Goals Allowed, Season
14—Philadelphia, 1973

Lowest Average Goals Per Game Allowed, Season
.74—Philadelphia, 1973

INDEX

Alberto, Carlos, 18, 33, 48
Ali, Muhammad, 32
All-Star team, 34, 47, 98
American Conference, 19; Central Division, 19, Eastern Division, 19, Western Division, 19
American Soccer League (ASL), 12, 108
Anaheim, California, 38
Anderson, Dave, 17
"Apprentice footballers," 46; duties, 46
Aquinas High School (St. Louis), 39
Argentina World Cup team, 49, 50, 51, 55
Arsenal Club (North London), 101
Atlanta Apollos, 14
Atlanta Chiefs, 13, 19, 108
Atlantic Conference, 108
Attendance, 8, 9, 13, 17, 19, 21
Australia World Cup team, 48
Austria World Cup team, 48

Backing up, 100
Ball, 24, 56
Ball control, 22, 29, 53, 75, 76, 77, 78, 86, 90
Baltimore Bays, 14
Baltimore Comets, 14
Bandov, Boris, 55
Banks, Gordon, 96, 97, 98
Bauru, Brazil, 24
Beckenbauer, Franz, 17, 18, 50, 81, 89, 90, 91, 92, 98
Belgium World Cup team, 49
Belo Horizonte, Brazil, 51, 53
Best, George, 17, 92, 93

Bodonczy, Nico, 113, 114
Boston, Massachusetts, 17
Boston Beacons, 14
Bradley, Gordon, 22, 30
Brand, Jack, 66
Brandeis University, 39
Brazil World Cup team, 25, 27, 35, 48, 51, 53, 75, 97, 102, 103, 104
Brazilian soccer, 17, 24, 30, 53, 102, 103, 104
Brooklyn, New York, 96
Brooklyn German-Americans, 11
Brooklyn Hispanos, 12
Brown University, 38
Budd, Brian, 55, 86

California Clippers, 14
California Surf, 19, 38, 54, 86, 87
Canada World Cup team, 54, 55
Canadian soccer, 36, 37, 55
Cannon, Otey, 40
Carew, Rod, 40
Catenaccio system, 103, 105
Cawston, Merv, 83
Center circle, 59
Chicago, Illinois, 50
Chicago Mustangs, 14
Chicago Slovaks, 11
Chicago Spurs, 14
Chicago Sting, 19, 61, 76, 83
Chile World Cup team, 51, 53
Chinaglia, Giorgio, 17, 23, 87, 88, 89, 106
Chip pass, 86
Cleveland Browns, 26
Cleveland Shamrocks, 11

Cleveland Stokers, 14
Coaching, 24, 38, 40, 41, 43, 44, 45, 108-115
Coker, Ade, 74
College draft, 37, 38, 39, 46
College soccer, 11, 38, 39, 71
Colorado Caribous, 19, 86
Concentration, 14, 109, 110, 111, 114
Connecticut Bicentennials, 14
Connell, Mike, 93
Corner kick, 55, 58, 60, 62, 63, 70
Cosmopolitan League, 12
Cosmos, 4, 8, 16, 17, 18, 19, 20, 21, 22, 23, 26, 28, 29, 30, 32, 33, 34, 37, 38, 39, 44, 45, 48, 53, 54, 81, 89, 90, 92, 106, 111, 113, 114
Cruyff, Johan, 105
Cubatao, Brazil, 24

Dallas, Texas, 15
Dallas Tornado, 19, 29, 35, 36, 40, 86, 108
Darrell, Gary, 35
David, Steve, 86, 87, 88
de Brito, Valdemer, 24
Defense, 43, 54, 62, 63, 65, 66, 67, 70, 77, 78, 81, 94, 95, 107
Defensive tactics, 81, 106, 107
Dempsey, Jack, 17
Denver Dynamos, 14
Derby, England, 10
Detroit Cougars, 14
Detroit Express, 19, 35, 87, 88
Die Fussball-Weltmeisterschaft, 47
Direct free kick, 64, 65, 66, 81
do Nascimento, Celeste, 24

do Nascimento, Edson Arantes. *See* Pelé

do Nascimento, Edson, Jr., 33

do Nascimento, Joao Ramos (Dondinho), 24

Downing Stadium (New York), 29

Dribbling, 21, 22, 43, 56, 77, 78, 79, 82, 86, 90, 99, 100, 105, 107

Dutch whirl, 104, 105

Edwardsville, Illinois, 38

El Campeonato del Mundo de Futbal, 47

El Salvador World Cup team, 47, 67, 68

England, Mike, 94, 95, 98, 100

England World Cup team, 48, 49, 51, 53, 79, 96

Englewood, New Jersey, 89

English soccer, 10, 28, 30, 34, 45, 48, 49, 51, 53, 79, 96, 108, 114

European Nations Cup, 91

Fall River, Massachusetts, 50

Federation Internationale de Football Association (FIFA), 11, 48, 49

Finney, Tom, 51

Firmani, Eddie, 30, 37, 38, 90, 113

Flater, Mike, 55

Florissant Valley Community College, 38

Ford, President Gerald, 17

Foreman, Chuck, 40

Formations, 85, 99, 100, 101, 102, 103, 105

Ft. Lauderdale Strikers, 4, 8, 19, 38, 79, 92, 96, 97, 108, 109, 110, 111, 112, 113, 114, 115

Foul, 64, 81

Fowles, Colin, 109

France World Cup team, 25, 49

Free kick, 41, 55, 64, 101

Gabriel, Jim, 43, 44

Gaetjens, Joe, 51

Game film, 21, 110

Gant, Brian, 78

Gardner, Paul, 29, 41, 51

German-American Soccer League, 12, 54

German Football Federation, 49

Giants Stadium, 4, 31, 92

Goal, 25, 33, 51, 55, 56, 58, 65, 70

Goal area, 67, 84

Goal crossbar, 51, 57, 67, 68, 77

Goal kick, 60, 63, 64, 70

Goal line, 54, 56, 62, 63, 97

Goal mouth, 29

Goal net, 55, 58, 59

Goal post, 51, 57, 67

Goalkeeper, 22, 50, 55, 56, 57, 58, 60, 63, 64, 65, 66, 67, 70, 72, 77, 83, 84, 96, 100, 101

Gosling, Dr. Herman, 25

Graham, Otto, 26

Great Britain, 51

Griffiths, Clive, 76

Grgurev, Freddy, 54

Guadalajara, Mexico, 97

Guadalupe school (Seattle), 43

Harris, Ron, 92, 93

Hartford Italians, 11

Hartwick College, 38

Harvard University, 11, 67

Heading, 27, 29, 44, 45, 51, 55, 56, 66, 79, 80, 82, 88, 97, 100

Hendrie, Paul, 31

Herberger, Sepp, 91

High school draft, 38, 39

High school soccer, 11, 41, 45, 46, 59, 71; coaching, 41; rules, 41, 59

Hofstra University, 9, 12

Holland World Cup team, 47, 52, 104

Honduras World Cup team, 47

Houston Hurricane, 19

Houston Stars, 14

Hudson, Ray, 79

Hungary World Cup team, 26, 48, 102

Indirect free kick, 68

Indoor soccer, 71, 72, 73; court size, 71, 73; soccer rules, 71, 73

International coaching, 41, 46

International soccer, 17, 20, 22, 24, 25, 27, 30, 34, 35, 36, 37, 38, 40, 46, 48, 49, 52, 53, 100, 104, 105

Irving, David, 8

Italy World Cup team, 49, 50, 51, 89, 103

Jackson, Reggie, 40

Jagger, Mick, 32

Jairzinho, 97

Johannesburg, South Africa, 93

Johnstone, Jimmy, 44

Jones, Bobby, 17

Jules Rimet Trophy, 27, 47, 53

Kansas City Spurs, 14

Kearny (New Jersey) Irish, 12

Kickoff, 45, 51, 59

Kingston, Jamaica, 67

Kissinger, Henry, 32

Klivecka, Ray, 37

Krol, Rund, 52

Lamm, Kurt, 27, 91, 92
Las Vegas Quicksilvers, 14
Leeper, Curtis, 109
Lewis, Cleveland, 39
Lindbergh, Charles, 49
Linesmen, 58
Lockhart Stadium, 8, 98
Los Angeles, California, 17
Los Angeles Aztecs, 17, 19, 87, 88, 92, 96
Los Angeles Skyhawks, 108
Los Angeles Toros, 14
Los Angeles Wolves, 14

Machin, Mel, 94, 95
Madison Square Garden, 12
Maier, Sepp, 50
Makowski, Greg, 38, 39
Manchester United, 92
Manhasset, New York, 12
Marseille, France, 47
Martin, Eric, 82
Matthews, Stanley, 51, 52
Mausser, Arnie, 54, 55, 96
Mazzei, Julio, 27, 28
McAlister, Jim, 20, 43, 44, 45, 95
Melbourne, Australia, 47
Memphis Rogues, 19
Meramec Community College, 38
Messing, Shep, 33, 67, 68, 82, 95, 96
Mexico, 53
Mexico World Cup team, 54
Miami, Florida, 87
Miami Gatos, 14
Miami Toros, 87, 108
Miller, Al, 36
Minnesota Kicks, 19, 55
Morgan, Joe, 40
Muller, Gerd, 52, 104
Munich, Germany, 47, 49, 67

Namath, Joe, 16
National Basketball Association (NBA), 40
National Conference, 18, 19; Central Division, 19; Eastern Division, 19; Western Division, 19
National Professional Soccer League, 13
Netherland World Cup team, 49
New England Tea Men, 19
New Jersey Americans, 12
New York, N. Y., 8, 9, 12, 50, 115
New York Generals, 11, 14
New York Greeks, 12
New York Jets, 16
New York Mets, 16
New York Post, 38
New York Times, The, 9, 17, 40, 41
Newman, Ron, 38, 97, 108, 109, 110, 111, 112, 113, 114, 115
Numbering system, 85
North American Soccer League (NASL), 8, 9, 12, 13, 14, 15, 16, 17, 18, 19, 20, 27, 30, 34, 36, 38, 39, 40, 41, 43, 44, 45, 54, 56, 69, 71, 84, 85, 86, 87, 89, 96, 97, 99, 108, 109, 115

Oakey, Graham, 78
Oakland Clippers, 14
Oakland Stompers, 19, 67, 82, 95
Offside line, 69
Offside trap, 101
Offside violation, 58, 68, 69, 70, 101
Olympic Games, 48, 67
Olympic Stadium (Munich), 47
Olympique de Montreal, 14
Oneonta, New York, 38
Out-of-bounds play, 60

Paraguay World Cup team, 49
Passing, 21, 29, 56, 75, 77, 80, 86, 95, 100
Pedro, John, 35
Pelé, 16, 17, 18, 19, 20, 21-23, 45, 53, 75, 87, 96, 98
Penalties, 64, 65, 66, 68, 81
Penalty area, 63, 66, 107
Penalty kick, 66, 67, 81
Philadelphia Fury, 19
Philadelphia Spartans, 14
Philadelphia Ukranians, 12
Pinel, Marcel, 49
Pittsburgh Phantoms, 14
Playing positions, 85, 89, 90, 91, 92, 99, 100, 105; defenders, 85, 90, 91, 93, 95, 99, 100, 105; forwards, 85, 89, 99, 100, 105; goalkeeper, 85, 99, 100; midfielders, 85, 90, 91, 92, 99, 100
Point Fortin, Trinidad, 87
Pope Pius XII, 22
Port-au-Prince, Haiti, 54
Portland, Oregon, 8
Portland Timbers, 19, 31, 78
Portugal, 35
Princeton University, 11
Punting, 84

Queen Elizabeth II, 79

Redford, Robert, 32
Referee, 58, 59, 65, 68, 70, 82
Referee cards, 68, 69
Ridley Park, Pennsylvania, 96
Rigby, Bob, 96
Rimet, Jules, 27
Rio de Janeiro, 47
Robert F. Kennedy Stadium, 21
Rochester Lancers, 9, 19, 35

Romania World Cup team, 49
Rome, Italy, 50
Rote, Kyle, Jr., 35, 36, 86, 96
Rule infraction, 58, 68, 69
Rules, 11, 41, 56, 57, 58, 59, 60, 63, 64, 65, 66, 67, 68, 69, 70, 80, 81, 82, 84, 101

St. Louis Stars, 9, 14, 38
St. Louis University, 38, 54
San Diego, California, 9, 14, 19
San Diego Sockers, 19
San Diego Toros, 14
San Jose Earthquakes, 16, 19
Santos of Brazil, 17, 24, 27, 28, 30, 32, 33
Scoring, 18, 19, 56, 57, 58, 62
Scotland, 35, 49, 100
Scouts, 44, 110
Screening, 78, 79
Seattle Community College, 44
Seattle Sounders, 8, 19, 20, 30, 34, 40, 43, 44, 55, 94, 95
Seaver, Tom, 16
Sewell, John, 38
Shooting, 21, 22, 77
Shoot-out, 57
Shoulder charge, 81
Simpson, O. J., 40
Skills, 22, 24, 25, 26, 30, 41, 45, 75-84
Skotarek, Alex, 61
Smethurst, Derek, 34
Smith, Bobby, 53, 54
Soccer Bowl, 8, 19, 30, 44
Soccer clinic, 28, 29
Soccer field, 41, 42, 43, 44, 46, 56, 57; size of, 41, 42, 43, 56
South America, 11, 13, 30, 47, 49
Southern Illinois University, 38, 39
Spain, 47

Spain World Cup team, 28, 49, 50
Speed, 22, 86, 87, 90
Strategy, 22, 43, 62, 65, 67, 68, 110
Streisand, Barbra, 32
Strenicer, Gene, 61
Substituting, 41, 52, 59, 60
Super Bowl, 16
Sweeper, 103

Tackle, 22, 81, 82
Tampa Bay Rowdies, 16, 19, 30, 34, 39, 54, 71, 93, 96
Tarantini, Alberto, 55
Team Hawaii, 14
Television, 13, 14, 15, 17, 29, 40, 44, 48, 53, 56, 86
Thring, J. C., 11
Throw-in, 58, 60, 70
Tilden, Bill, 17
Timing, 57, 58, 59, 80, 82
Tipping, 83, 97
Topps Chewing Gum Company, 9
Toronto Falcons, 14
Toronto Metros, 19
Touchline, 55
Toye, Clive, 17, 27, 28, 30
Training, 9, 30, 38, 41, 45, 46, 85, 86, 89, 97, 112, 114
Trapping, 22, 25, 45, 74, 75, 77, 79, 82, 100
Tres Coracoes, Brazil, 23
Triestina, 103
Trinidad, 34, 35
Trost, Al, 54, 55
Tulsa Roughnecks, 19, 35

United Nations, 47
United States, 11, 12, 13, 14, 17, 71, 92, 114
United States Football Association (USFA), 12

United States Soccer Association (USSA), 13
United States Soccer Federation (USSF), 12, 27, 40, 91
United States World Cup team, 27, 48, 49, 50, 51, 52, 53, 54, 55
University of San Francisco, 38
University of the South (Sewanee, Tennessee), 36
Uruguay World Cup team, 48, 49, 51

Van Der Beck, Perry, 39
Vancouver Royals, 14
Vancouver Whitecaps, 19
Volley, 77

Warner Communications, 17
Washington Darts, 14
Washington Diplomats, 19, 21, 35, 71, 78, 82
Washington Whips, 14
Webster, Adrian, 34
Wales World Cup team, 13, 25
West Germany World Cup team, 28, 34, 35, 47, 51, 52, 53, 90, 91, 92, 104
Wilner, Roy, 21, 22
Wilson, Bruce, 55
Wolf, Dave, 40
Woosnam, Phil, 9, 13, 14, 19, 27
World Cup tournaments, 25, 26, 27, 47-55, 75, 91, 97, 98, 102, 103, 104

Yale University, 11
Yankee Stadium, 11, 12
Yasin, Erol, 34
Yugoslavia World Cup team, 35, 49

Zaire, 47
Zec, Ninoslav, 35